AN
TO THE CHRISTIAN DIVORCEE

An Open Book
to
THE CHRISTIAN DIVORCEE

Roger II. Crook

Broadman Press
Nashville, Tennessee

Library of Congress Catalog Card Number: 73-87064
Dewey Decimal Classification: 301.428
Printed in the United States of America

This book is neither an attempt to justify nor to condemn divorce.
Its purpose is to offer practical help to the growing number of divorcees.

CONTENTS

Foreword   vii

1. The Best Way Out?   11

2. Before Your Divorce   23

3. Your Emotional Adjustment   31

4. Your Religion and Your Divorce   51

5. Your Social Adjustment   71

6. Your Children   93

7. Your Divorce and the Law   115

8. Remarriage?   137

Epilogue   157

FOREWORD

As a Christian who is divorced, you find yourself in a totally unexpected situation.

You were taught, and you believed, that marriage is ordained of God and is intended to be a permanent relationship. You expected that your marriage would last. Divorce, you assumed, was something that happened to *other people*—people who did not choose their mate wisely or who did not have the spiritual resources with which to meet the inevitable problems of marriage. But it was something that would never happen to you.

Yet it has happened to you. Since you never expected it, you were completely unprepared for it. You were taken by surprise when you realized that your marriage had deteriorated to the point that there was no hope for it. Now, bewildered and disillusioned, you have to pick up the pieces of your life.

Although you are a Christian, you may not have received much help from your church in handling the problems associated with your divorce.

Perhaps that is because the church ignores you. It busies itself with teaching the ideal of marriage as a permanent union. It encourages its young people to marry and provides religious sanction for their union by performing wedding ceremonies. It sets up Sunday School classes for "married young people." It celebrates the birth of children and provides for their religious instruction. Indeed, the church seems oriented toward a family program "from the cradle to the grave." But in that program you may be left out.

Perhaps it is because you are not quite sure what is your standing with the church. Like all other Christians, you have tried with varying degrees of success to live out your faith. Even though you have not always been successful, you have felt at home with those other people who have not been successful either. Now your problem is not simply something that you have done or failed to do; it is something that you are: *a divorcee.* Where do you stand with all those people who are still husband and wife? How is the church going to interpret Jesus' teachings about divorce? How is it going to apply the exhortations of Paul? Do you really belong?

The church may not help you think through what has happened and what the future holds. Although it helped you get married, it perhaps cannot help you as a divorcee. It helped you understand what was happening to you as you fell in love; it seems unable to help you understand what happened as you became disenchanted with your marriage. The church that seems to have the answers to the problems of suffering and bereavement and pain and worry and fear does not seem to have the answer to the problem of disillusionment and failure in marriage.

In this book we begin with the assumption that some Christians do fail in their marriage and secure a divorce. This attitude is apparently different from that which for so long prevailed in the church. In the past the church has regarded divorce as a sin and warned its people not to resort to it.

But Christians are divorcing—and are doing it in increasing numbers. Some who divorce their mates may be Christian in name only. Many others, however, are Christian in fact—committed to the God whom they have come to know in Jesus Christ, faithful in their participation in the life and work of his church, honest in their work, concerned about the needs of others.

In this book we shall try to look at the problems of the Christian divorcee. Many of those problems he shares with people who are not Christian, although for him they are complicated by the fact that he looks at them from a Christian perspective. Other problems grow out of his failure to achieve the ideal which he sees to be Christian. The Christian divorcee tries to come to grips with all these issues, not simply in terms of what he wants to do, but in terms of what is the right thing to do. He tries to relate his actions to the will of God.

It is this Christian perspective that is the distinctive characteristic of this book. We do not quote Scripture as the answer to every question, although we do examine biblical teachings wherever they are appropriate. As a matter of fact, many of the problems of the modern divorcee were not anticipated in the Bible. There is, however, a basic Christian approach to personal problems, and that is the approach which we try to take here. We want to discover what is the right course of action for the Christian whose marriage has disintegrated.

1. THE BEST WAY OUT?

DEAR DR. CROOK:

My child and I are now located—temporarily—with my parents in Atlanta. As I told you in my note earlier I am going ahead with the legal action necessary to end my marriage. I left our house with Anne, Monday, January 29th. I had stayed awake all night out of fear—George had told me he would kill my parents, accused me of having an affair with our dentist (I had to see him Sunday morning for a severe gum infection), gone through my purse and taken checks, car keys, etc., and then slipped something—I don't know what—under his pillow when he came to bed. There is much more, but this is what prompted my action. I believe that George is very sick—he was to see a psychiatrist this morning. He has begged me, through my attorney, my parents, aunts, uncles, brothers, etc., to come back and make my own terms. I cannot. I do not look forward to what sort of life is ahead for Anne and me now, but I know for certain that I could not endure another moment living with George.

He is aware of where I am now and has been instructed by both attorneys to leave me alone. The four of us (George, me, and the attorneys) met together a week ago in an attempt to make some steps toward a legal separation agreement (either oral or written) and George literally went to pieces after about 5 or 6 minutes. The next conference is scheduled for 30 days from last Monday.

I will have to be back and forth between here and there. On one of these trips I would like to see you. I will call or write first.

Sincerely,

SUSAN

Five years earlier, at the end of her sophomore year in college, Susan had dropped out of school and married George, a public-school teacher. After the birth of their daughter they began to have trouble. She sought counseling from her college faculty adviser on several occasions. Twice earlier she had left George, but neither time was away for more than three days. This time, however, the separation was permanent and ultimately the divorce was granted.

Susan had entered college with the thought of preparing herself for some church-related vocation. Now she is a divorced woman with a small child, struggling desperately to complete college, dependent upon her parents, wondering if there is now any place for her in the church, shattered by her sense of personal failure, troubled with feelings of guilt, and not quite sure of how or why things ever reached this point.

Bill is a successful attorney. He and Sharon were married for twenty years and had two sons, the oldest of whom was a high school senior. They were quite active in their church, were respected in the community, and gave the impression of being a typical middle-aged couple. Before Sharon was aware that Bill was contemplating divorce, however, he had made all his plans. He rented an apartment and then announced to his family that he was moving out. There was no other woman involved. There was not any unusual conflict between him and Sharon. He was simply tired of the way things were and wanted a different way of life. A year later they were divorced, and six months after the divorce was final Bill married someone else. Both Bill and Sharon continue to attend church services, though with much less regularity than before.

Shortly after his graduation from the seminary, Frank and Ellen were married. He had accepted the pastorate of a small, rural church. Three pastorates and twenty-two years later, Ellen divorced Frank and married a professional man, also divorced, who was living in the same town. Frank confided to a friend that he had known three months after he and Ellen were married that it was a mistake. He was content to spend his entire career serving small churches, while she was a very ambitious person who wanted her husband to move up in ecclesiastical circles.

Joe met Mary Anne when he came to town working with a surveyor. A high school drop-out and a veteran of the Korean conflict, he was a heavy drinker and prone to violence. Her family was closely identified with the church, her father a deacon and her grandfather a minister. She was a waitress in a cafe in the small town. Three months after they met they were married and he took her back to his hometown. They had two children whom Mary Anne regularly took to Sunday School and church. Joe's drinking increased, his employment became more and more irregular, and he became more and more abusive of his wife and children. She left him twice, then returned. The third time the separation was permanent.

One of the last issues of the now-defunct *Life* reported:

One evening nine months ago, 35-year-old Wanda Lee Adams, college graduate, wife of a middle-level Seattle executive and mother of three, walked out on her family to begin a new life on her own. There was no great animosity then, nor is there now. No dramatic grievances existed, and by most standards the 14-year marriage was a success. Her husband Don was considerate, attentive and devoted. Money was not a factor. The problem was that somewhere around her tenth year of marriage, Wanda Adams had begun to see her life as increasingly frustrating and suffocating. She started to work again and enjoyed it. She went back to school and there encountered the women's liberation movement. 'I then realized,' she says, 'that I was experiencing what a lot of women experience. Don was a decent human being who had allowed me to grow to a certain point. But past that point I had to leave.' And she did.[1]

How Did It Happen?

You are not alone. It is happening to a great many people—good people. It is happening for good reasons or for poor reasons or for no reasons at all. It is happening more and more often. Today one divorce is granted for every two to three marriages contracted. The story of each divorce is different, and there is no such thing as a typical one. Although your story may be similar in some ways to that of someone else, it is yours and yours alone.

"I take thee . . . for better, for worse," says the traditional marriage ceremony. Making those promises, you had no idea how bad that "worse" might be. You believed that your marriage would last. You did not necessarily expect a bed of roses. Yet you were confident that your love would be enough to hold you together no matter what happened. You believed that marriage was intended by God to be a permanent relationship, lasting "until death us do part."

Your marriage began with joy and with the expectation of personal fulfillment and happiness. You loved each other with a love that was perhaps blind and foolish, but that was nonetheless real. You committed yourself to one another "before God and this company." But now it is all over.

What happened? Did you break up, or did you just drift apart? By one means or another, you reached the conclusion that you "just don't love each other any more." Something has destroyed your love, and life together is no longer possible. What was that something? Maybe it was disillusionment.

Perhaps you saw in your partner—or your partner saw in you—or each saw in the other—something that had never before been apparent. Were there some annoying personal habits? Did you discover that certain attitudes became increasingly hard to live with? Did you find that things were expected of you that you were unable or unwilling to do? Did you realize one day that you had lost your own identity? Did you discover that you were missing out on some of the best things of life?

Perhaps it was simply the end of the courtship. When you were falling in love and later when you were making your plans for marriage, you tried hard to please each other. You put your best foot forward. Even in the early part of the marriage you were anxious to make each other happy. Married life, however, cannot be one eternal honeymoon. Did you become tired of always trying to please your mate? Did you sometimes feel that you were being taken advantage of? In the "give and take" of marriage, did you reach the point where there seemed to be more "give" than "take"?

Maybe a part of the difficulty, at least, was the failure of one—or both—of you to fit into the roles of husband and wife. Both in terms of relationships with one another and in terms of relationships with the community at large, the fact of marriage makes a big difference. It is granted that these roles are largely cultural matters. They are not innately male and female characteristics so much as they are attributes that our society has assigned to husband and wife. But we do live in society. We are pressured by society to fit those roles. Society largely determines what a wife may expect of a husband and a husband of a wife. And now we do expect those things. If the husband or wife, however, does not meet those expectations, there may be real frustration.

Perhaps you and/or your partner were dissatisfied in the area of sex. It is very difficult to nail down a problem in this area, because sex is so closely tied in with everything else in the husband-wife relationship. Most of the time, a couple's sexual adjustment will be good if they are well-adjusted in other areas of life, and a poor sex relationship often reflects poor personal adjustment. Yet, since sex is a basic part of our lives and since we all come to marriage with rather well-defined attitudes toward sex, a basic conflict in this area will affect adversely a couple's total relationship.

Could it be that there was one serious problem which could not be resolved and which ultimately had to wreck your marriage? Was your spouse an alcoholic or a chronic gambler? Maybe one or the other of you had an uncontrollably violent temper, or maybe your spouse could never free himself of his parents.

The basic source of difficulty may have been something external to the marriage. One of you may have become involved with a third person. Such involvement, it should be admitted, is not likely to occur if the marital relationship is deeply satisfying. But if there is not that satisfaction at home, a man or a woman who finds himself associating closely at work or in some other way with an overwhelmingly attractive person may find himself drawn into a romantic involvement in spite of himself. Many marriages which were not really strong have been shattered in just this way.

As you think about the cause of the break-up of your marriage, remember one important fact: The specific cause that you cite may have been only the trigger. The marriage itself may already have been an explosive situation just waiting for something to set it off. Had not this development done it, something else probably would have.

The Larger Setting

While it does not solve your immediate problems, it may

help in the long run if you are aware of a number of factors in our society which conspire to make success in marriage difficult. They do not explain entirely the failure of your marriage. Yet they do help you understand what happened to you and a knowledge of them may help you adjust to the situation.

One of those factors is the changing status of women. Enjoying a new freedom that began to be more of a reality in the early 1960's, women became much more visible and vocal in every area of life. An increasing percentage of them are graduating from college, and an increasing percentage of them are finding employment outside the home. No longer are they restricted to factory work and the "lady-like" professions of teaching and nursing. They are executives, scientists, engineers, publishers, doctors, lawyers, and even ministers. Some work out of economic necessity, some work to supplement family income in order to afford certain luxuries, and some work because they want a career. More and more they are becoming involved in politics, both in running for office and in campaigning for persons and causes. This increased involvement in education, in employment, and in politics is giving to all women a greater sense of independence. It is opening up to them greater possibilities of finding personal fulfillment in something besides marriage and child-rearing.

Although this greater independence of women can be a plus for marriage, it is often a problem. When everyone understood that the man was the head of the family, that he was the breadwinner and that his wife was the homemaker, that his career came first, that while he had many proper interests outside the home she centered her interests in the home, then people could fit into their roles with a minimum of difficulty. When the stability of a marriage, in other words, depended chiefly upon husband and wife fitting into well-established and clearly defined roles, success was fairly easily achieved. When those roles are no longer taken for granted, however, and when harmony in marriage depends upon the adjustment of two independent persons to each other, it is much more difficult to achieve.

One of the chief sources of difficulty in marriage, at this point, is the decreasing importance of the home to both men and women. Increasingly both men and women center their thinking on their work. A working person spends eight hours a day—more or less—on his job. Having devoted all his mental and physical energies to one thing all day, he finds it difficult to turn those energies in another direction when he gets home. A teacher or plumber is a teacher or plumber at home as well as on the job. This tendency is not new. It has always been the case. But where the eight-hour daily stint moves husband and wife in opposite directions, problems for the marriage are created.

A second social factor that affects all of us is the changing sex practices and standards. Whether or not we have been faithful to our ideals, most of us have subscribed to the traditional teaching of the church that sexual intercourse is a marital relationship, and that whatever tends to "lead to" premarital intercourse is to be discouraged. We have bemoaned the double standard which has been more harsh on women who violated the ideal than on men who did so. But we are in the midst of a sexual revolution which is quite vocal in challenging the ideal. More effective methods of contraception and the ease and relative safety of abortion make it a whole new ball game. Without necessarily accepting them, Christians cannot but be affected at least a bit by the thoughts of those who advocate a much freer attitude. Although we may not agree with them, we are almost inevitably made a little less sure of our own position. And we are a little less sure of what the marital relationship is.

Another factor is the change in the law that reflects a change in our customs. Increasingly the law is regarding both marriage and divorce as a purely personal matter, and the tendency is to say as little as possible about who may or may not marry and under what circumstances marriages can be contracted. On the one hand, though there have been no significant changes in the laws regulating marriage, more and more people are questioning the propriety of requiring a formal contract (which is what marriage is in the eyes of the law) between two people who wish to live together. And on the other hand, there is apparent a trend toward the granting of divorce by mutual consent.

In more than a dozen states it is now possible to be divorced simply on the ground of having lived apart for a specified length of time. In 1970 California began a radically different approach to the legal dissolution of marriage.[2] The law of that state now requires no plaintiff and no defendant and no allegation of misconduct. All divorce proceedings are heard in family courts and marriages are dissolved upon the finding of "irreconcilable differences" or of incurable insanity. During the next decade or so most of our state legislatures undoubtedly will deal with a reformation of the laws of marriage and divorce. It seems clear that divorce will become easier. Whether we are aware of it or not, we are affected by this spirit of complete freedom of personal decision.

Where Do You Go from Here?

As a Christian whose marriage has been terminated by divorce, you are in a dilemma. On the one hand, besides the desire shared by Christians and non-Christians alike for a happy and enduring marriage, you are aware of the Christian ideal of a permanent union of a man and a woman. "Those whom God hath joined together let no man put asunder," your ceremony probably said. But on the other hand, your marriage did in fact deteriorate until it became intolerable either for you or for your mate or for both. Now it is over. You may have a deep sense of regret. You may feel guilty. You may be plagued by doubts about yourself. You may have serious problems of finances, care of children, personal relationships with family and friends, even questions about your faith in God and your place in the church.

Perhaps divorce is the best way out of an intolerable situation. Perhaps it is forced upon you in spite of the fact that you do not want a divorce. But where do you go from here?

According to Morton M. Hunt, you move into a different world, what he calls "The World of the Formerly Married." Separated and divorced people, he says:

are part of the overall American culture and interact with its members on its own terms; but elsewhere they have a private and special set of norms that guide them in their interactions with each other, and from which they derive their own customs, moral values, rules of fair play, and devices for coping with the problems special to their condition.[3]

In this new world, says Hunt, you will learn very quickly to identify other formerly married people. You will learn "an unpublished body of rules of behavior" governing all kinds of situations: behavior with old friends, both married and unmarried; the formation of new friendships; dating; explanations to children; and personal conduct in private and in public.

The FM man or woman learns not to harp on his or her recurrent bouts of despair or loneliness; it bores and finally estranges the married friend. Equally, however, one learns not to reveal much of the surging feeling of renewal, the delight in freedom, the joy and pride of rediscovered sexuality; such confessions are disturbing to the married, and bring disapproval and even the loss of friendship. One learns not to dwell too often upon problems with the children, the ex-spouse, or the former in-laws; friends listen and sympathize, but behind their kindly replies there often lurks an unuttered rebuke: "You needn't have had these troubles. . . . *You* chose to make them for yourself, we chose to remain in marriage." [4]

As you face this new and unknown world there is no one to introduce you to it, to explain the rules to you, to offer answers to your questions. You will learn on your own how to live as a divorced person. You will have emotions which are yours alone. You will face problems that are unique to your situation. You will adjust in your own way to the new limitations and the new freedoms. In the chapters that follow, you will find some suggestions that may be of value to you as you make the transition.

Notes

All Scripture quotations are from the Revised Standard Version.

1. *Life,* March 17, 1972, p. 34b.

2. For a full description of this plan, see Aidan R. Gough, "Divorce Without Squalor," *The Nation,* January 12, 1970, pp. 17-20.

3. Morton M. Hunt, *The World of the Formerly Married* (New York: McGraw-Hill, 1966), p. 5.

4. *Ibid.,* pp. 708.

2. BEFORE YOUR DIVORCE

If you are contemplating a divorce, you ought to be aware of one very important fact: although divorce may be your best possible alternative in an extremely difficult situation, it will not solve all your problems.

Before you decide that divorce is the only avenue left for you, you need to do some careful thinking about what success and failure in marriage are. In other words, how do you know that your marriage is a failure?

Success or Failure?

Happiness is the thing we want most from marriage. Few people are so naive as to believe that they can marry and "live happily ever after." Yet we make happiness the supreme goal in life and measure success in everything in terms of our relationship to it: education, work, possessions, recreation, religion, and family experiences are all expected to contribute to our happiness. If they do, then we consider ourselves a success in those areas. If they do not, then we consider ourselves a failure in those areas. When this test is applied to marriage, we are apt to conclude that if we are happy, then nothing else matters. If we are not happy, however, then nothing else can compensate for that fact.

Although happiness is properly one criterion of success in marriage, it is hardly the only one and perhaps not even the most important one. As a matter of fact, the pursuit of happiness is the most disappointing thing we can undertake. Happiness is a by-product of our activities rather than a goal to be sought. In terms of marriage, happiness is the result of a mutual commitment of husband and wife to each other and to certain values. If it comes at all, it comes as a consequence of their common devotion.

It is important to think clearly also about the nature of happiness in marriage. It is not the same as the happiness that accompanies the romance of young love, the newness and adventure and intense emotion (highly charged with sex) that characterizes the courtship and the honeymoon. All emotions fluctuate, and romance is at heart emotional. In marriage at its best these emotions are replaced by acceptance, by security and commitment, by the deepening of the relationship. These latter qualities, while not as exciting as romance, are nevertheless more productive of true and enduring happiness because they are not so dependent upon external circumstances.

In addition to evaluating success in terms of happiness, you would do well to think in terms of the basic functions of marriage. One of the two basic functions of marriage is the procreation and rearing of children. This is not to suggest that the childless marriage is necessarily a failure. It is to suggest, however, that the couple who are providing for their children the kind of environment that will help them become strong, stable, mature individuals are succeeding in their marriage in one of the most significant possible ways. No matter how happy a couple may be, if in any way they are warping the lives of their children, they are failing in their marriage.

The other basic function of marriage is the enrichment of the lives of the husband and the wife. In marriage it is not intended that a man and a woman lose their identity as individuals. Rather each should become more fully and completely a person. A good marriage serves to open up to both partners possibilities of personal development unknown outside of marriage. Each partner contributes to the developing personality of the other. If a marriage helps a husband to be a stronger man and a wife to be a stronger woman, then it is in a significant sense a success. Naturally this kind of development does not occur when husband and wife are at each other's throats all the time. Neither does it occur when they ignore one another. If it occurs in any way, however, then there is hope for the marriage.

"Success" and "failure," of course, are relative terms. Who can say that he is absolutely happy or that his children have absolutely the right kind of home environment or that he and his mate are enriching the lives of each other in absolutely the right way? There may be such a thing as absolute failure—though that is doubtful. There certainly is *no such thing as absolute success.* In contemplating divorce, you have to weigh successes and failures without benefit of any scale which can tell you clearly what you ought to do.

The Best Alternative?

Are you now certain that divorce is the best alternative open to you? As a Christian you want to do what is best for yourself, for your children if you have any, and for your mate. All of you are involved in this situation. All of you want certain basic satisfactions in life. All of you have certain needs. All of you want to be happy. It may be that no matter what happens all of you will be hurt. However you have tried, you need to raise the question again, Can we possibly save our marriage? Can we do more toward helping all of the persons involved achieve their goals by finding alternative solutions to our problems?

Many years ago Edmund Bergler insisted, in his book by that name, that *Divorce Won't Help.* [1] His thesis was that in nearly every instance of divorce the real problem was not between husband and wife, but personal problems of the individuals. Those problems, he said, persisted even after the marriage was terminated. They would plague the individual no matter whether he remained married, or divorced and remained single, or divorced and married someone else. He recommended that the individual contemplating divorce face up to himself and deal with those personal problems rather than trying to escape by getting out of a difficult situation that was the result rather than the cause of the problem.

Bergler probably overstated his case. Many people have found that even if divorce did not solve their problems it improved their situation. If you have not yet taken the step of divorce, however, it might be well for you to take a good, long look at yourself. If it is true that the failure of your marriage is due even in part to your own personality or attitudes or fears or aspirations, then you might be able, even at this late date, to salvage your marriage. And if you can do so, you will go much further in achieving your goals in life than you are likely to do in terminating your marriage.

If you have decided on divorce, you are admitting that your marriage is sick and that you see no possibility of recovery. But what have you done to try to save your marriage? Do you know what the real problems are? Have you honestly looked at yourself? at your mate? at your relationship? What evidence do you have that divorce will solve your problems? Has divorce solved the problems of your friends who took this approach?

Divorce *may be* the best alternative that is open to you. Before you proceed with your plans, however, you need to be sure. Just as a sick body can sometimes be healed, so can a sick marriage. You don't tear down a house just because the roof leaks, or trade automobiles because of a dent in a fender. On the other hand, a house may have deteriorated to the point that it is a waste to try to repair it, and an automobile may be a complete wreck. Can your marriage even yet be saved? Or is it beyond redemption?

Because of your intense emotional involvement, you probably have difficulty in thinking clearly about this question. When we consider any problems in which we are involved, we tend to distort the facts by defensiveness, by self-deception, by rationalizing. If you have not sought outside help, it would be well at this point to consult your minister or a marriage counselor who can help you look carefully at the situation and help the two of you reach some decision as to what is best for everyone concerned.

If you decide that divorce is in fact the best possible solution to your extremely difficult situation, that is not to say that it is what you *want* or even that it is the *right* thing. What you want is a good marriage. In ideal terms, that is what is *right.* That is no longer an option for you, however. At the time that you married that possibility was open to you. Different decisions then might have enabled you to move toward that goal. If you had married a different person, for example, you might not now be divorcing your spouse. Of if you had been more mature when you married, or if you had tried harder to understand each other, or even if you had been a little wiser in the way you acted, this might never have happened. But all of that is now past, and things have now reached the point where the ideal is no longer possible to you. That option of "living together happily ever after" is no longer open. With things as they are now, as much as you regret it, a divorce may be the best way out of this impossible situation.

A New Status

If it develops that divorce is the best course for you to follow, however, you should not expect that step to solve all

your problems. Many divorced persons find that divorce has
not rid them of their biggest problem, since that problem lay
not in their mates but in themselves. We always tend to blame
the failure of our marriage on the other person. *He* is the
alcoholic, or *she* is the nag. *He* is unfaithful, or *she* is unrespon-
sive. There is always an element of truth in such accusations,
of course. But there is always another side. And that other
side—the responsibility that is yours—may be of dimensions
that it will give you trouble no matter what happens.

By divorce you will be restored legally to the status of a
single person. The obligations to your mate which were a part
of your marriage contract will no longer be there. But the
past cannot be undone. You have been deeply affected by your
marriage. At one time you found certain satisfactions in it,
and those satisfactions helped to shape your personality. Those
satisfactions gave place to dissatisfactions, and you have been
deeply hurt by the deterioration of the relationship. You will
not come out unscathed. The marks of this failure will not
be the determining factor in either failure or success in the
rest of your life. But they will be there and will exert their
influence.

If you have children, your return to the status of a single
person will be even more difficult. I am speaking here not
of the practical considerations of child care and finances, but
of the effect that parenthood has upon you. Whether you have
custody of your children or whether your former spouse does,
they are still *your* children. You have been changed by becoming a parent, and you can never undo that change even if
you want to. If you have custody of the children, you are
tied down in a practical way. You have total responsibility
for planning their food, clothes, and shelter. In addition, you
have the sole responsibility for their healthy emotional, intel-
lectual, and spiritual development. If your mate has custody

of the children, you suffer bereavement in their loss. Even visiting rights do not make up for that loss. The divorced person with children is still, in a sense, "married."

All human beings need both to love and to be loved. Doubtless you did not find that need to be fulfilled in your marriage. Because you probably married for love and you expected your marriage to meet that need, you may now be more keenly aware of that need than ever. Divorce takes you out of a marital relationship that was not meeting this need. It does not put you into a situation in which it will be met any better.

If you have decided that divorce is the best possible solution to your problems, you owe it to yourself, to your mate, and to your children to make every effort to see to it that all of you come out of the experience as unharmed as possible. It may be possible for you to have what Sherwin calls a "compatible divorce." [2] The lines of communication between you and your mate may be sufficiently open for you to make plans calmly, to respect both the needs and the wishes of each other, and to avoid making the children choose between loving father and loving mother. If you can do this, while you will not come out of the experience unscathed, the hurt will be minimized.

A divorce is final. It closes the door completely to a chapter in your life. It is saying, "The marriage is over and done with; it is dead." Before you take that final step of divorce, therefore, you might do well to try a separation. I am not here talking about that legal separation which in many states is a ground for divorce. I am referring rather to an agreement between you and your mate that before you take any legal steps to terminate the marriage, you will try living apart to determine whether that is really what you want and need. You may in fact find that life is much better for you this way. If, however, you find that it is not better but worse, then you will know that there has to be some alternative to divorce as a solution.

As you plan for your divorce, you will need to give attention to many of the things which we are discussing in this book. Your own emotional involvement will make it difficult if not impossible for you to think rationally about them alone. Doubtless you will be discussing some of these matters with friends. But they will not likely meet the need for counseling, for they too are emotionally involved. They may be *your* friends, or *your mate's* friends, or may not want to choose sides. They will be more inclined to agree with whoever talks with them rather than to raise pertinent questions and make helpful observations. It would be far better for you to talk with your minister, or with a professional marriage counselor, who may be able to help you think clearly about issues and implications.

In *The Divorced Mother*, Carol Mindey has a chapter on "What Every Divorcee Needs." While her comments are addressed to women, the items she discusses, with some adaptation, are equally applicable to men.[3] These items are: a sense of humor, a job, good health, good teeth, reliable car, an education, a bank account, and the ability to take over.

This listing clearly reflects Mrs. Mindey's own personal experiences as she was married at the age of twenty, divorced at the age of twenty-nine, and remarried at the age of thirty-six. Although the items seem almost self-evident, the list calls attention to the fact that there are many very practical considerations to which most people give very little attention. If the list does nothing else, it says to you, You must consider some other matters than the simple fact that you are unhappy in your marriage and want out.

Notes

1. Edmund Bergler, *Divorce Won't Help* (New York: Harper. 1948).

2. Robert Veit Sherwin, *Compatible Divorce* (New York: Crown. 1969).

3. Carol Mindey, *The Divorced Mother* (New York: McGraw-Hill. 1969) pp. 40-52.

3. YOUR EMOTIONAL ADJUSTMENT

I have never known a divorced person for whom the experience of getting the divorce was not a crisis. It does not seem to matter whether a person divorces his mate or is divorced by his mate. It does not seem to matter whether the divorce is contested or uncontested. It does not seem to matter whether the person wanted the divorce. It does not seem to matter whether one or both of the marriage partners sought counseling before the divorce occurred. It seems always to be a traumatic experience.

Why is it so?

When two people have lived together over a period of time they have really become a part of each other. They may fight like cats and dogs on the one hand. Or on the other they may have an "armed truce" in which they have as little as possible to do with each other. It is not likely, however, that they can live in the same house and be completely indifferent to each other. They have to adjust their lives to the comings and goings of each other. They share the living room, the kitchen, the bathroom, if not the bedroom. They have mutual friends. They may attend church together. However difficult their relationships may be, they *are* relationships. The two are a part of the lives of each other.

When a part of your life is taken from you, you have to adjust emotionally to that fact. It is an intensely emotional experience, for example, to change jobs, or to move from one city to another, or even to move from one house to another. We grieve when a member of our family dies—even one who has lived far away for many years. If our world is disrupted for any reason, we find it something of an ordeal to adjust to the change, no matter how welcome the change may be.

The Agonizing Reappraisal

Whether you plan to do so or not, you probably will engage in what has been called an "agonizing reappraisal." You will be asking yourself, "What went wrong? Why did things happen as they did? What kind of person am I? What does the future hold? How can I be sure that now life will be better?" You will be experiencing unexpected and unpleasant emotions. You will react to situations in ways that are surprising to yourself and·to your friends. If you do not deliberately and consciously deal with these matters, they may force themselves into your subconscious and influence your actions and reactions in an adverse way.

As unpleasant as it is, you will be dealing with the fact that you have failed. We never like to admit failure in anything. We prefer to think that we can succeed at anything we undertake. If we fail, we want to place the blame somewhere. If, for example, we did not pass a course in school, we say that the teacher didn't know the subject matter, or that he could not explain it clearly, or that the subject was not interesting, or that we simply did not study hard enough. Rarely will we admit that we tried our best and found that our best was not good enough. The failure has to be someone's fault—either someone else's or our own—and that fault can be corrected if we put the effort to it.

If we have to admit that we tried our best and failed then we place the blame on factors that are completely beyond our control. Other forces, we say, combined to make impossible the achievement of the task we undertook. We did everything humanly possible to make a program go over, for example, but the other people involved did not do their part. The failure is therefore not our fault.

Because marriage is so important, it is extremely difficult for us to admit that we have failed to make a go of it. The decision to marry someone is perhaps the most important single decision a person makes (with the exception of his decision to follow Christ). On the decision to marry so much else hinges. It affects education, career, personal development, religion, social relationships, family relationships, and so on. Having made that decision, therefore, and having tried very hard to build a good marriage, your divorce seems to bring your whole life to the brink of disaster. Little wonder that you want to avoid acknowledging the fact of failure.

A failure your marriage has been, however, and the sooner you acknowledge that fact the better off you are. Divorce is not what you had in mind when you said, "For better for worse, for richer for poorer, in sickness and in health." You intended a permanent union that was not merely a legal contract or a social arrangement, but a real oneness. And that oneness does not now exist.

In assessing responsibility for the failure of your marriage, then, this human tendency to pass the buck comes to the fore. You want to place all the blame on your husband or your wife. He left you. Or she behaved in such a miserable way that it became impossible for you to live together any longer. He drank too much or became involved with someone else or had a violent temper. You tried your best to make your marriage work but got no cooperation. You are innocent, and he is guilty.

The fact of the matter, however, is both of you share in the responsibility for the failure of your marriage. You may not share equally. One of you probably carries the greater portion of the blame. But without doubt each of you is guilty of some offenses against the other and against the union. At times each has been a problem to the other. That is the case even in successful marriages, for no one can manage the intimacies of marriage without ever offending the other. A valid assessment of your failure, therefore, must involve a facing up to your responsibility in it.

In this reappraisal you should not merely look at the marriage that failed. Indeed there is little value in looking to the past unless you relate the past to the present and the future. You have given up on your marriage. What you are now concerned with is yourself in your present situation and yourself and your future. A look at the past is important only insofar as it helps you understand and adjust to your new situation.

You may find it impossible to handle this reappraisal alone. Most of us are simply incapable of the kind of objectivity that will let us see in ourselves our own weaknesses or our own inadequacy or our own guilt. You will do well to talk about your situation with a minister or with some other counselor. Your friends will be of help to you, and we shall say more about this in a bit. They cannot serve this function, however, because they are friends. They cannot be adequately objective. You need to talk with someone not emotionally involved with you who has some training and experience and who can help you see things clearly.

The Painful Emotions

The most difficult problem is not the rational questions to which accurate answers may be found. Rather it is the emotions with which you have to struggle and which are not subject to rational control. An awareness of what feelings you may expect to have and a rational look at them, however, might make the situation a little more tolerable.

Grief

Surprisingly enough, you are likely to experience a sense of grief. Surprising because your friends may tell you that you are really much better off without that mate with whom you were so unhappy. You may even have been telling yourself that a great burden has been lifted from your shoulders and that you are now free to be the kind of person you could never be so long as you had to contend with the problems of your marriage.

Grief is emotional pain experienced as a result of great loss. It is usually associated with bereavement. It takes place with any extended separation, however—separation related to business or military responsibilities, or to children growing up and leaving home, or to divorce. It is not unlike the emotion of anxiety which you feel when you face the loss of something important to you: loss of job, failure in business, demotion at work, sometimes even moving from a home that you have occupied for some time.

Grief does not depend upon something being unexpected or unplanned for. It may in fact be associated with something that we have long anticipated—or even wanted and planned for. All that is necessary to produce grief is the loss, or the threatened loss, of something or someone emotionally significant to you.

Grief, then, is most commonly associated with death. It occurs in connection with divorce because, in a real sense, a divorce is the death of a marriage—or at least the burial of a marriage that has already died. However extreme may have been your unhappiness in your marriage, that unhappiness was a part of your emotional world. You may not have enjoyed your quarrels and fights—or your stony silences. They were a part of your world, however, and they were intimately tied in with the rest of your emotional world. Now that those experiences are over, you have to rearrange your whole life. In time you can do it. But it will take time.

Grief is considered normal in the case of bereavement. As a matter of fact, no matter how unpleasant may have béen our relationships with the one who died, we are expected to idealize him. We are supposed never to speak evil of the dead. That expectation, by the way, often causes problems. No one is ideal, and most of us remember some bad situations and unpleasant incidents associated with the deceased. We are ashamed to admit that we remember those things, however, and try to pretend that those thoughts do not cross our minds. Even if we acknowledge that our relationships with the deceased have been extremely unpleasant, however, we still experience some grief. A part of our world has been wrenched from us. We are genuinely sorry.

Grief is not considered normal in the case of divorce, however. You are supposed to be happy now that the affair is over. Consequently you are puzzled and perhaps even a little ashamed when you grieve over the loss of a mate who is still living and whom you have come to detest. After all, you have been telling both yourself and your friends that you are not to blame for what has happened, that it is your spouse who is responsible for the turn of events, and that you did everything you could to make your marriage work. Now that it is over, it doesn't seem logical that you should miss him so much.

Emotions are so deep-seated and powerful that they cannot be completely controlled and repressed. In the case of bereavement, crying is one of the most common and expected, and therefore acceptable, means of expression. Since the grief of bereavement and the grief of divorce are essentially the same, therefore, it should not surprise you if you cry a bit over what has happened to you and to your marriage.

You may express your grief in other ways. You may lose yourself in the business of your work and/or home responsibilities. You may find yourself unnaturally breezy and excitable. You may talk too much—or too little. You may become physically ill. You may be depressed. You may have trouble sleeping. You may lose interest in what is going on around you and perhaps have trouble concentrating. You may be easily irritated and always tired. You may try to "drown your sorrow in drink." You may try to lose yourself in a whirl of social activities.

Not all of these activities are necessarily the expression of grief alone. After all, our emotions are a complex; they are not isolated feelings. We rarely do anything on the basis of one emotion alone. The element of grief is likely to be involved in your reactions, however, and it is best for you to recognize it, accept it as a normal experience, and find appropriate and helpful ways of expressing it.

Normally your grief can be expected to diminish with the passing of time. As the intensity of the emotion diminishes, your body and your mind will begin to function normally. In the case of bereavement the process usually takes six weeks or so. In the case of divorce, because of the bitterness involved and because of the lack of recognized ways of expressing it, the process may take longer. In time, however, you may expect your grief to pass. As you talk about the situation, and as you involve yourself in the necessary decisions and actions for your new way of life, healing will occur.

Guilt

Another emotion which you are likely to experience is a sense of guilt. As a Christian you have been taught, and you have honestly believed, that marriage is a permanent institution. You meant it when you said, "For better for worse, for richer for poorer, in sickness and in health, until death us do part." You took seriously the exhortation, "What God has joined together, let not man put asunder." And now you are divorced. However necessary that divorce may have been, the question haunts you: Am I going contrary to the teaching of the Bible?

In another chapter we shall give attention to the teachings of the Bible which are relevant to marriage and divorce. At this point the problem is your feeling of guilt and the proper way to deal with it.

At the outset you need to sift out your feelings. Do not confuse guilt with grief or frustration or loneliness or anxiety or any of the other painful emotions. They are related in your experience. The one may intensify the other or overlap with the other. Perhaps as you handle these other emotions you will also be dealing with your feeling of guilt. But you need to face directly and honestly any sense of guilt which you may have.

You should deal with your sense of guilt for the failure of your marriage in exactly the same way you deal with the guilt in other areas of life. The first thing is to acknowledge your responsibility for the failure. Though that responsibility is not yours alone, it is yours in part. If you are looking for some way to say that the situation was entirely beyond your control, then you are refusing to accept your share of the responsibility. As difficult as it is, you need to say: This is what I did wrong, and that is what I should have done that I did not do.

In your acknowledgement of your responsibility, you should recognize that your offense is not just against your marriage partner but also against God. It is he who ordained marriage. It was before him that you made your marriage vows. It is his purposes for you that have been thwarted.

In your confession to God you do not pass on to him any information that he does not already have. You do not need to inform him of what has happened. You do open yourself up to his forgiving and cleansing work, however. Confession is not needed to persuade God to receive you; it is needed only to open yourself up to his healing work.

Having confessed to God and sought his forgiveness, you need agonize no longer over your guilt. Although you will continue to be troubled with other painful emotions, guilt need no longer complicate them. Forgiveness is a reality. It does not have to be begged for. It does not have to be earned. It does not depend upon your conduct. It is the gift of God's grace. He does in fact remove the barriers between you and him. The reality of forgiveness is your greatest resource for dealing with the other painful emotions which you feel.

Wounded Pride

One of the biggest emotional problems which you face is the damage to your own pride. When the economic and social and religious problems have been dealt with adequately, the insult to the ego for having failed in this most important of human undertakings remains. This is especially true when it was your mate who sought the divorce, for then the impression is left that in some important way you were inadequate. Or that your partner found someone whom he preferred to you. It may even make you wonder whether there is something about you that is lacking, whether you are capable of a satisfying relationship with anyone.

Wounded pride is usually a greater problem for women than for men. Whether properly so or not, in our society men and women are given their identity in very different ways. We think of men in terms of their work. A man is a "rich man, poor man, beggar man, thief; doctor, lawyer, merchant, chief." We generally identify women, on the other hand, in terms of their family. A woman is "Mrs. John Smith." She may or may not work outside the home, but it is her family that tells who she really is. Not only does the general public think this way; this is the way a woman is likely to think of herself. Consequently, when her marriage disintegrates, she may feel that she is losing her personhood. Although this way of thinking is unjust, it is a fact with which we must reckon.

Suppose a man leaves his wife because he is involved with another woman. What questions flood his wife's mind? Why did she lose his love? Is she no longer attractive? Is she sexually inadequate? Did he ever really love her? Is it her fault that she is no longer able to hold him? How can she face the humiliation of being abandoned for someone else?

On the other hand, what questions plague the man who leaves his wife? Why has his wife grown cold toward him? Why does she no longer try to please him? Has he failed her? Even though he has taken the initiative to leave, is it his fault that the marriage which entered so happily turned sour? How can he explain to his friends, to his employers, even to himself the fact that he became involved with another woman?

The wound to your pride is not necessarily all bad. It may help you to get a better understanding of yourself. Such a self-understanding in turn may be the key to a happier and more successful life. Divorce is a difficult way to be forced into that understanding. You did not choose this as the best way to attain that goal. Yet if self-understanding is an unintended result, it can be one of the good things that comes out of a bad situation. Whether you divorced your mate or whether your mate divorced you, you can use this experience to discover who you really are and to make yourself a better person.

Loneliness

Most newly divorced persons experience for a time an intense loneliness. How long the period of loneliness lasts varies, of course, with the person and with the circumstances. Almost always, however, it is a serious problem.

The problem of loneliness grows out of having to change from thinking in terms of "we" to thinking in terms of "I." In the early months of marriage the reverse was the problem. A part of the process of marital adjustment is this merging of two lives. It involves everything about a person: work, religion, social activities, meals, the bedroom, the bathroom—everything. It is a difficult adjustment, and rarely is it perfectly achieved, even in the most successful marriage. Even in the worst marriage, however, that adjustment is made at least in part. In time it becomes a part of the subconscious so that we are not even aware of the extent to which it has been effected.

When a person is divorced, he has to reverse that process. Suddenly he is all alone, without all of those relationships of which he had not even been fully aware. Even the period of growing alienation prior to separation did not prepare him for being alone. Even the period of separation before divorce did not do it. Married people sometimes complain of too much togetherness. Divorced people experience too much aloneness.

Not all people experience the sense of loneliness to the same degree. If you wanted the divorce you may not feel it quite so much as you would if you did not want the divorce. At first, in fact, you may feel vastly relieved at not having your unwanted partner around. When you want companionship, you can turn to your friends. In the long run, however, you probably will find that even being with friends whenever you wish does not provide the kind of companionship that will genuinely relieve loneliness. And you will find that at times no friend is available. You will spend many hours in solitude.

The problem forces itself upon you when you get off from work. When you come home you are greeted by emptiness. You prepare your meal and eat alone. Television becomes boring and reading seems pointless. You spend the evening alone and you sleep alone. If you try to find distraction at a restaurant, a movie, a bar, you soon find that that is all it is—a distraction, not companionship. Perhaps you have children to care for. If so, they only delay the problem until you have fed, bathed, and bedded them. Then the loneliness sets in.

Of course, you were alone before you were married and you did not feel this way. Marriage changes you, however. It profoundly affects your very being, whether you are aware of it or not. Your divorce cannot return you emotionally to a premarital status. You once did love; you once did have a companionship that is unlike that which you have had with your parents and unlike that which you have with your children. Having known that companionship, even imperfectly, you miss it in a way that is impossible to those who have never been married.

The psychologists call this loneliness of the divorced person "role disturbance." You have functioned as husband or wife, and have become accustomed to doing so. Now you can no longer fulfill that role. If you are separated from your children, you have the additional problem of being barred from functioning as a parent. Even visitation rights do not permit you to be a parent in the full sense. Sooner or later it becomes apparent to you and to your children that you are, in fact, a visitor. However great or little were your personal satisfactions in the marital and parental roles, when they are taken from you their absence creates a void.

You may feel that you have this problem pretty well under control, only to be brought face to face with it again. Your wedding anniversary comes around, or a birthday, or a holiday—and you are flooded with memories. A child makes a comment or asks a question. Or you hear a song that had special meaning. Or you encounter an old friend. In time you get this problem under control, but it does take time. Even long after the divorce, perhaps even after you have married someone else, memories may sometimes cause pain.

I once was talking with a divorced man about joining the church of which I was pastor and it became apparent that his divorce was still a painful subject for him. More than ten years earlier he had come home from the military service and shortly thereafter began proceedings to divorce his wife on the ground of living apart for a year. He insisted that he had what he called "biblical grounds" for divorce, but he did not make that kind of charge in the courts because it would have been "messy." Three years after his divorce he married again and had a good marriage. But the scars from that earlier ill-fated marriage were there. The visit of a pastor brought them to the surface again.

If you are separated and planning to be divorced, your loneliness may lead you to attempt a reconciliation. As you try to talk to your estranged partner in a calm and polite fashion about the children or about property arrangements, you may think, "Perhaps we could make a go of it if we tried again." Indeed, many people have separated for a time, then got together again, and made a success of their marriage. Others, however, have tried it and found that they still could not live together.

Your loneliness may lead you to idealize your former partner. You may begin to remember the good times the two of you had together and may begin to think that the bad times were really not quite so bad. Those offensive habits or attitudes may now seem rather insignificant after all. That drinking problem may not have been as serious as it seemed at the time. You may have driven him (her) into that extramarital affair by your own lack of warmth. You may remember the love for the children, the endless hours spent with them, the hard work and personal sacrifice for them.

This idealization of your former mate is no more likely to be a valid assessment of the situation than is your picture of that person as totally bad and entirely responsible for the failure of your marriage. It may help you, however, to move on to a more balanced view of the situation—of both yourself and your former partner. The time will come when you will be able to make an objective judgment as to what was good and what was bad about your marriage, and to make some decisions about yourself and your future that will enable you to profit from even this unhappy experience.

Like all other intense feelings, your loneliness will wear off if you let it. The void in your life created by your separation from your husband (wife) will in time be filled. You will rearrange your way of doing things: of eating and sleeping and working, of caring for the children, of social life. You may find your new life as a single person quite rewarding. You may eventually remarry and have a good marriage with a new partner. You can, of course, make a fetish of your loneliness. You can feed on it, perhaps even enjoy it. But you do not have to keep yourself permanently miserable because of what has happened. The secret of a happy life, married or single, is your involvement in life and in the world around you.

How can you deal with your loneliness? You should be very cautious at this point, for there are many ways of dealing with it that are dangerous and destructive. Some people seclude themselves and feed upon their loneliness, avoiding all human contact except what is absolutely necessary. The result is a sicker and sicker personality. Others go to the opposite extreme, clutching at every opportunity to be with other people, desperately clinging to friends and relatives—as if they are afraid to be alone. Some people suddenly begin to spend money lavishly and even irresponsibly. Others turn to drink. Others rush headlong into new romantic relationships—trying to find someone—anyone—to replace the partner who is gone.

Although your friends can be of great help to you in handling loneliness as in handling other emotional problems, they cannot take this burden from you. You will have to come to grips with it for yourself. You will have to draw upon your own inner resources. The road which you travel will not be easy because loneliness is painful. As time passes, the ache can be expected to become less acute. When it strikes you, however, you cannot ignore it. How you respond to it will determine whether the experience destroys you or makes you a stronger and better individual.

Anxiety

A degree of anxiety about the future is likely to be tied in with all these other emotions. Will you be able to be both father and mother to the children? Or, if your former mate has custody of the children, can you survive with only occasional contact with them? How will your friends react to the situation? How will your work be affected? How will you handle your sex drive? How will you manage all of those things that you have been accustomed to having your wife or your husband do for you—however unwillingly?

Your anxiety will have to do not merely with such practical matters, however, but with your own self. You may be plagued with self-doubt growing out of this failure of your marriage. Are you capable of success? Could you have made a go of it with anyone? Is there something about you which makes you incapable of either giving or receiving love? Do you have the inner resources for dealing with serious problems?

What Now?

All of this has been said about common emotional reactions so that you might know what to expect. But now that the problem has been stated, where do you go from here? Is there anything that can be done to keep these problems from arising or to make them less dangerous and destructive? How can you deal with them?

Having read thus far, you have already taken the first step. There is no substitute for understanding what is happening. You know that what you feel is not at all unusual, but is a common experience for those who go through the ordeal of divorce. Although not every person has all of these emotions, most divorced persons have most of them. Furthermore, however intense they are at the moment, they will almost certainly pass in time. Soon you will be in better control.

Emotions must be expressed in some way. If you do not find appropriate and helpful ways, they may erupt in some way that will be dangerous and destructive either for yourself or for the people around you. If you are moved to tears, do not be surprised or ashamed. Tears are no less appropriate and helpful in the case of divorce than in the case of bereavement. If you feel that you have to talk to someone—anyone—that too is entirely appropriate provided you are careful about your choice of a person. When that person listens sympathetically, you can pour out your emotions without fear of criticism or betrayal of confidence. You can even be unconcerned about how your statements sound or whether they make sense. You need not worry about whether what you say represents everything that you feel, or whether you will always feel that way. You can express hostilities and regrets, self-condemnation and self-justification, hopes and fears all in the same breath. The important thing is that your pent-up feelings be expressed so that your inner pressure may be relieved.

A word might be said here about the help of your friends. They will probably sense your need at this time and will be there to help you. Their help will not be in what they say;

you may not even remember that. The fact that they are there to listen when you want to talk, or to sit with you in silence when you don't want to talk, is what you need. If you have such friends, call them when you are lonely or anxious. Express your concern about your own responsibility or your questions about your own sufficiency. Or just say, "I need you." Your friends will be there.

Insofar as possible, you will be well-advised to keep up your normal activities. Your life has already been seriously disrupted by the termination of your marriage. Additional stress may have been imposed by your having to move to a new place of residence. You may be separated from your children as well as from your mate. You may have to lose contact with some of your friends. The more changes you have to make at once, the greater the stress and the greater the problems. So go about your accustomed work. See those friends with whom you can maintain contact. Keep involved in your social and/or civic club activities. Keep up your church relationship. A radical rearrangement of your life is inevitable. The difficulty of that rearrangement will be increased with every additional adjustment that has to be made.

The sooner you are able to establish a new routine for your life the better off you will be. In spite of our love of adventure, we also love security. Security comes with the familiar. Involve yourself regularly, therefore, in activities that will demand your time and attention. The fact that you were married, with the demands that marriage made on your time and energy, closed the door to certain interests and activities for you. Being with your spouse made it impossible for you to follow certain interests that you had before you were married. Open now those doors and become involved in a new way. Your old self-image as a married person must be replaced by a new self-image. What that image is to be you will determine by the interests and activities to which you give yourself.

These interests, if they are to do for you what you desperately need, must be real. That is to say, there is no help for you in busying yourself about unimportant things just to have something to do. Mere distraction does not suffice, for it does not last. You can be distracted for the moment, only to face your loneliness and emptiness when next you are alone. Real interests, however, can help you because in giving yourself to them you are freed from the tyranny of yourself.

What kind of interests will do this? For many people it turns out to be their job. For others, it is involvement in a service activity. It may be the development of latent talents for art or music or drama or writing. It may be the cultivation of friendships, perhaps with people whose lives are empty and frustrated. There is a world of activities and interests, organized and unorganized, to which you may turn. What it is for you will depend upon what you find in yourself that needs developing. Certain possibilities of self-development and self-expression that were open to you as a married person are now gone. But now new options are open to you, and you will set the pattern for a new way of life.

In deciding on the pattern, beware of those dangerous escape mechanisms. Carol Mindey, in *The Divorced Mother,* speaks of some women who try to escape "by indulging in ultimately self-defeating and self-destructive activities." She lists such things as "dating 'wrong' kinds of men"; "having indiscriminate sexual affairs"; "spending most of their free time dating and searching for the 'right man' "; "spending money recklessly"; "socializing too much; finding escape in drinking; use of drugs, such as pep pills, tranquilizers, or sleeping pills"; and throwing herself into her work, "spending too much time away from home, almost as much as a man does." [1]

Our bodies tend to be self-healing. They try very hard to

throw off disease and to heal wounds. In most instances they succeed if we give them time. Sometimes the disease does some permanent damage, and sometimes the wound leaves a scar. Even in those instances, however, we can adjust and be reasonably strong and healthy.

In much the same way our spirits tend to be self-healing. Your unsuccessful marriage has seriously hurt you, and the trauma of separation and divorce may have scarred you. But in time your spirit will again be strong and healthy. No matter how difficult things may seem now, and no matter how stormy your emotions may be, in time you can expect a stability that will make life worthwhile.

Notes

1. Mindey, *op. cit.*, pp. 199-200.

4. YOUR RELIGION AND YOUR DIVORCE

"What therefore God has joined together, let not man put asunder," said Jesus (Mark 10:9).

But it has in fact been put asunder, either at your initiative or at that of your marriage partner. Was it wrong for you to be divorced?

As a Christian you have been taught all your life—and you have believed—that marriage is a lifetime proposition. Yet your marriage did not last a lifetime. How does the fact of divorce affect your religion? How does your religion help you now?

You are a part of a society that makes happiness the supreme criterion of success in marriage. If a couple are not happy, it is generally agreed, they should not remain together. Your own divorce, in fact, may not be due to any one specific crisis or problem so much as to a pervading unhappiness that one or the other—or both of you—felt. Does your acceptance of society's attitude and acting upon it mean that you have rejected your religious convictions? Does it mean that now you have no religious resources for dealing with this crisis?

The Bible

It is only in fairy tales that people marry and live happily ever afterward. So far as we have been able to discover, every human society has tried to regulate marriage with the expectation that marriage is a permanent arrangement. Every society, however, has also made provisions for the dissolution of unions that fail.

As Christians, we turn primarily to the New Testament, and specifically to the teachings of Jesus, for guidance. The New Testament, however, reflects its Old Testament background. To understand what the New Testament teaches, therefore, we must look first at the appropriate Old Testament material.

The Old Testament

In the Old Testament there is only one law regulating divorce:

When a man takes a wife and marries her, if then she finds no favor in his eyes because he has found some indecency in her, and he writes her a bill of divorce and puts it in her hand and sends her out of his house, and she departs out of his house, and if she goes and becomes another man's wife, and the latter husband dislikes her and writes her a bill of divorce and puts it in her hand and sends her out of his house, or if the latter husband dies, who took her to be his wife, then the former husband, who sent her away, may not take her again to be his wife, after she has been defiled (Deut. 24:1-4).

According to this law, a man could divorce his wife, but a woman could not divorce her husband. This situation is entirely in keeping with the traditional Semitic conception of the wife as, in a sense, the property of her husband. Since she belongs to him in a way in which he does not belong to her, he may quite properly dispose of her under certain conditions.

The conditions under which a man might divorce his wife were subject to debate.[1] What constitutes "indecency" in a wife? Strictly speaking, the term does not necessarily refer either to unchastity at the time of marriage or to unfaithfulness in marriage, since the prescribed penalty for both of these offenses was death (cf. Lev. 20:10; Deut. 22:24). The Old Testament does not record a single instance of this penalty being imposed, however, and in the Talmudic law it was removed. Adultery was commonly understood to violate the basic nature of marriage and was adequate reason for divorce. "Indency," therefore, was usually interpreted to refer to sexual offenses.

In actual practice, however, the most common ground for divorce was the barrenness of the wife. At certain periods in Hebrew history the problem of childlessness was solved by the husband taking either a concubine or a second wife. The alternative of divorce was open, however, and it was not unusual for a man to divorce his wife for this reason.

Since the law gave no guidance as to what constitutes indency, it is not surprising that divorce came to be permitted to the Hebrew husband for a wide variety of reasons and was quite easily obtained. The Old Testament does not indicate that any man lightly put away his wife. By the time of Jesus, however, due in part to Greek and Roman influences, divorce, though not widespread, was more common.

The divorce process was simple. The husband merely presented his wife with a "bill of divorce" and sent her away. Under some circumstances he was required to return the dowry to her family. Once that was done, the relationship was terminated. The woman might then quite properly become the wife of another man.

In spite of the ease with which a man could obtain a divorce, the practice was not common. In neither the Old Testament nor the New is there much evidence of divorce. Extra-biblical material from the New Testament period indicates that it was not unknown. Yet the Jewish family of the first century was quite stable.

In Jesus' day, the implications of the law regulating divorce were being debated. For some time the injustice of making no legal provision for a woman to terminate an intolerable marital relationship had been recognized and provisions had been made whereby she could take legal steps to force her husband to divorce her. The debate now centered on the question of what constituted indecency, and what therefore was a valid ground for divorce. Rabbi Hillel and his followers interpreted the law quite liberally, permitting divorce for almost anything that displeased the husband. Most of the rabbis, however, disapproved of such easy regulations and approved of divorce only for quite serious matters. Some of them even limited the grounds to marital infidelity.

The Teachings of Jesus

In the New Testament Jesus is reported as having spoken about divorce twice. These instances are recorded in Matthew 5:31-32 and Matthew 19:3-9. The first passage is paralleled in Luke 16:18 and the second in Mark 10:11-12. In addition, Paul referred to Jesus' teaching on the subject in 1 Corinthians 7:10-11.

In his teaching on divorce, as on other matters, Jesus apparently preferred to take the positive approach rather than the negative one. When the Pharisees asked him, "Is it lawful to divorce one's wife for any cause?" (Matt. 19:3; *cf.* Mark 10:2), he answered in terms of the permanence of marriage.

Have you not read that he who made them from the beginning made them male and female, and said, 'For this reason a man shall leave his father and mother and be joined to his wife, and the two shall become one'? So they are no longer two but one. What therefore God has joined together, let no man put asunder (Matt. 19:4-6).

Only when pushed by the Pharisees did Jesus speak directly to their question of the permissibility of divorce.

They said to him, "Why then did Moses command one to give a certificate of divorce, and to put her away?" He said to them, "For your hardness of heart Moses allowed you to divorce your wives, but from the beginning it was not so. And I say to you: whoever divorces his wife, except for unchastity, and marries another, commits adultery (Matt. 19:7-9).

In the Sermon on the Mount Jesus commented on a number of Old Testament laws, including the one having to do with divorce.

It was also said, "Whoever divorces his wife, let him give her a certificate of divorce." But I say to you that every one who divorces his wife, except on the ground of unchastity, makes her an adulteress; and whoever marries a divorced woman commits adultery (Matt. 5:31-32).

When Mark reported Jesus' conversation with the Pharisees and with his disciples about divorce, he did not quote Jesus as saying, "except for unchastity" (Mark 10:2-12). Neither did Luke when he reported Jesus' teaching which parallels the statement in the Sermon on the Mount (Luke 16:18). An important question, therefore, is whether Jesus permitted divorce on the ground of unchastity. In both instances, Matthew reports him as having done so. Neither Mark nor Luke, however, records any exception to the teaching that marriage is not to be terminated by divorce. Paul's report of Jesus' teaching on the subject (1 Cor. 7:10-11) does not note any exception.

If Jesus made the exception, as Matthew indicates, then he came out solidly in agreement with the rabbis who interpreted "indecency" in sexual terms. If he did not, as Mark, Luke, and Paul indicate, then his interpretation seems even more restrictive than that of the most conservative of his contemporaries.

It seems logical to conclude that Jesus did not make the exception. The reasons for reaching that conclusion are: (1) The oldest records, those of Paul and Mark, do not report the exception. (2) If a change in the teaching of Jesus were made by a later disciple, as must have been the case in one report or the other since they do not agree, it seems more likely that a disciple would make a difficult teaching easier than that he would make a difficult teaching even harder. (3) Jesus usually taught not by giving rules but by stating ideals. If he permitted divorce on one ground, however, then this teaching has the quality of legislation. To say that there is one valid ground for divorce is to make a rule. To say that marriage is a permanent relationship is to teach the ideal. Had Jesus made the exception, like Moses he would have been permitting divorce for adequate cause in cases where people failed to live in accord with the ideal. The enactment of this ruling, however, would have been a concession to human weakness rather than a statement of what God intended for the man-woman relationship.

The Interpretation of Paul

In interpreting Jesus' teaching on divorce, Paul brought in a new element (1 Cor. 7:12-16). He did not approve of a Christian divorcing his unbelieving partner because of the difference in faith. Yet, should that unbelieving partner be unwilling to live with the Christian, said Paul, then the Christian is free. A believer cannot preserve his marriage by himself. While he should not take the initiative to divorce his spouse, should that spouse terminate the marriage then the believer is "not bound." Presumably this means that he is free to marry someone else.

The biblical ideal seems clear: marriage is intended by God to be a permanent union of one man and one woman. Life in accordance with that ideal is the most meaningful and satisfying possible way of personal fulfillment for most people.

But there is a problem. Moses, said Jesus, made a concession "for your hardness of heart." Perhaps Jesus did specify unchastity as the chief example. Are there other examples? Are there other offenses that make a marriage in effect no marriage? "Hardness of heart" was not limited to the ancient Hebrews. As a matter of fact, success in attaining the ideal seems far more difficult in our world than it was in biblical days.

Before looking upon your own situation in the light of the teaching of Jesus, it is important to consider what the church says and does about divorce.

The Churches

In all major religious groups divorce is regarded as coming short of the Christian ideal. In their statements on marriage, as would be expected, the churches always emphasize the permanent union of one man and one woman. In most instances, little is said about divorce per se, but a great deal is said about the remarriage of divorced persons. In the chapter on remarriage we will consider the appropriate statements. At this point, however, we need to see where the churches stand on divorce.

The Roman Catholic position is a simple one. The Roman Catholic Church considers marriage a sacrament. The true union of a man and a woman is created neither by the couple nor by the priest but by God himself. No man, therefore, can in fact terminate a sacramental union. Man cannot undo what God has done. *Canon 1118* says it all: "Marriage which is valid and consummated cannot be dissolved by any human power, nor by any cause save death."

Upon occasion the Roman Catholic Church does approve a couple being separated. It permits permenent separation on the ground of adultery *(Canon 1129)* and temporary separation for other reasons *(Canon 1131)*. The Church is unwilling to call this separation a "divorce," for it does not regard it as a termination of the marriage. Even if the persons so separated secure a legal divorce, in the eyes of the Church they are still married.

For practical purposes, however, it is incorrect to say that the Roman Catholic Church does not permit divorce. There is in fact no difference between a permanent separation and a divorce, since in neither instance can a marriage fulfill its functions. Although the Church says that a separated couple are still married, they do not live as a married couple. The point at which the Catholic Church differs from most Protestant churches, therefore, is not whether a couple can be divorced, but whether a divorced person is free to marry someone else.

It should be noted also that the Roman Catholic Church provides for the annulment of marriages under certain conditions. (Remember that an annulment by the Church has no bearing on the legal status of a marriage.) An annulment is a declaration that because it did not meet all the requirements of a "valid" marriage, a sacramental union did not exist in the case of the couple involved. The requirements for a valid marriage are spelled out in detail in *Canons 1067-1080*. The impediments to such a marriage include want of age, impotence, spiritual relationship, legal relationship, and the like. If one of these regulations were violated, then the marriage may be declared null and void. There is no way of knowing how many marriages the Roman Catholic Church annuls in any given year, but annulments are certainly not unknown.

For a long time most Protestant churches insisted that the only valid ground for divorce was adultery. This policy was not usually stated in a discussion of divorce, however, but in a discussion of the remarriage of divorced persons. The Canon Law of the Episcopal Church, the Discipline of the Methodist Church, and the Book of Church Order of both major branches of the Presbyterian Church permitted the remarriage of a divorced person only if he were the "innocent party" to a divorce on the ground of adultery. Although their church policy prohibits such regulations for denominations like the Baptists and the Disciples, most people in these groups also subscribed to this view.

Beginning about the time of the end of World War II, however, most Protestant churches began to revise their stand. The Episcopal Church was the first to do so, adopting a new Canon Law in 1946. By 1958 the United Lutheran Church, the Methodists, the Presbyterian Church in the United States of America, and the Presbyterian Church in the United States had all adopted new regulations. Without exception, the revisions liberalized the position of the churches. The practice and attitudes of Baptists and Disciples seem to have changed in the same way.

The present position of Protestants, for the most part, can probably be summarized thus: While divorce is discouraged, and while it is to be regretted whenever it seems necessary, the divorced person's relationship to the church is not jeopardized.

In some churches, however, as a divorced person you may find yourself a sort of "second-class" member. On the basis of the statement in 1 Timothy 3:2 and 3:12 that bishops and deacons should be "married only once" (RSV) or "the husband of one wife" (KJV), many churches prohibit divorced persons from holding these offices. By implication, that prohibition is sometimes extended to include the position of teacher in the Sunday School.

This interpretation of these verses is not the only possible one, nor is it, in my judgment, the best one. This phrase has been variously interpreted as prohibiting concubinage, polygamy, remarriage after divorce, and remarriage after death. It has even been interpreted to mean that the person holding one of these offices *must be a married man!*

In my judgment, this statement must be taken as a part of an overall description of the kind of person who is sought for a position of leadership in the church. This passage is most helpful if it is seen not as a set of rules but as principles for guidance. The church needs in positions of leadership persons of Christian character and devotion. The person who falls short of the ideal in one aspect does not thereby demonstrate that he is to be regarded forever thereafter as morally corrupt. He should not, for one failure, have closed to him all avenues of service to Christ and his church. At any rate, it hardly seems more appropriate to prohibit a divorced person from holding such offices than to prohibit someone who falls short on any of the other characteristics. The difference between a divorced Christian and one who is not divorced is *not* that one is a sinner and the other not. It is rather that their failures are of a different sort. All Christians should be guided by the ideals of Christian character, and none who genuinely regrets his failures should be excluded from using his abilities in the service of Christ.

Clyde Lee Herring has commented: "The principle emerges: Taken the present conditions of life, a Christian still should serve Christ to the best of his ability. Evidently, then, God still works with people as they are, even though he insists that his ideal is not lowered in the process." [2] Herring adds that divorced Christians are not generally people of low moral standards. They are Christians who in one significant aspect of life have fallen short of the ideal. They are still Christians, however, and they have a proper and important place in the Christian fellowship.

In no way does this interpretation minimize the seriousness of the problem of failure in marriage. Neither does it minimize the importance of offices in the church, nor does it lower the qualifications for holding office. What it does is to recognize that the literal enforcement of all the qualifications stated in the passage would disqualify nearly everyone. It holds before all persons those ideals of conduct by which we should govern ourselves.

The church quite properly tries to entrust leadership to the best qualified persons. To have a regulation, however, which bars a person who is in good standing from the church from holding an office is a bit hypocritical. It is to say, "You may have a limited membership in the Christian community. You may do this, but not that. You may worship. You may contribute your money. But you may not contribute your services."

Shirley Stephens once interviewed five divorced Christians, asking about their relationship to the church.[3] While it is not possible to generalize on the basis of the experience of five persons, we can see that the attitudes of divorced persons toward their relationship to the church vary. Apparently the relationship of these five varied not so much because of the practices of the churches as because of the attitudes of the individual divorcee. About one of the interviewees Mrs. Stephens said:

Nobody in the church does or says anything to make Jo Ellen feel unwelcome. Maybe that's the problem—the church doesn't do anything. "For the most part," Jo Ellen asserted, "the church acts as if divorcees do not exist. Ignore them, and they'll go away," she added, only half joking.

Such indeed may be the attitude of some churches. On the other hand, it may be merely the way one individual perceives the situation. About another interviewee, Mrs. Stephens reported:

When Candy became legally separated, she did not go back to the church where she had been a member. She was ashamed, and she did not want sympathy. Too well, she remembered whispered remarks overheard in her youth, "She's divorced." Candy moved to another city.

Of a third person, Mrs. Stephens said: "Cliff had not felt guilty, but he was conscious of the thoughts of other people about divorce." Yet another person had even stronger feelings:

"I felt divorce was a blot on me," Gay said. Abandoned by her husband, she went from another state back to her home church, though it was to face old acquaintances. She felt like a complete failure. Strongly opposed to divorce, she had, at the age of 22, resigned herself to living separated (without divorce) from her husband for the rest of her life and rearing her child alone. She joined the church choir but would not sing a solo. She did not think people would accept her singing as sincere.

The fifth person also had an almost traumatic experience:

After 15 years of marriage, divorce interrupted Bettie's life. For some time she would not teach a Sunday School class on a regular basis as she had done in the past. She was concerned that parents would object, and she was afraid that she would present a poor example to the children. Her feelings persisted even though she believes she had biblical grounds for divorce.

Questioned about the actual reactions of people in the church when the fact of divorce was made known, all five indicated that people were either "surprised" or "shocked," but none encountered any real hostility or rejection. Asked, "What place of leadership would you feel comfortable in?" only one said that she did not believe she could take a position of leadership.

The conclusion which I would draw from this information is that although church members generally are a bit uncertain as to what to think about divorced Christians, it is the divorced person himself who has the greatest confusion. That confusion may be based upon an observation of the relationship of other divorced persons to the church. It may be based also upon those mixed emotions which were discussed in the previous chapter. And it may be based upon the divorced person's belief both that divorce is "wrong" and that in this case divorce was necessary.

At this moment you are not likely to change the situation in your church. In the long run you may be able to help the church deal more helpfully with other divorced persons. Now, however, you are trying to come to grips with your own relationship to the church. The best thing you can do is to find your place in the church just as fully as you can. Find those Christian friends who are willing to receive you at face value. Use your talents and abilities in whatever ways are open to you. If you have continuing problems, go to your pastor about them.

A Theological Interpretation

In the light of the teaching of the Scripture and the practices of the church, let us now think about your divorce. What is your situation as a divorced Christian? Put another way, this means: How can you reconcile the fact that you are a Christian to the fact that you have deliberately taken a course of action that is different from the Christian ideal?

We must begin with the fact that throughout the Bible the ideal of a permanent union is upheld. The creation account says, "Therefore a man leaves his father and his mother and cleaves to his wife, and they become one flesh" (Gen. 2:24). Jesus quoted this statement with approval, and added: "What therefore God has joined together, let not man put asunder" (Matt. 19:5). Divorce is therefore a violation of the ideal.

It is important for us to ask, "Why did Jesus teach what he did? Why did he consider divorce to be wrong?" The answer to this question is to be found, at least in part, in an understanding of the place of women in Jesus' day. Women were totally dependent upon men. A woman depended first upon her father, and then upon her husband. If she were widowed, she depended upon her son. To divorce a woman, therefore, was to deprive her of all security. Except in rare instances, she owned no property. There were no careers open to her by which she could earn her own living. She had to have a man to care for her. If her husband were to divorce her, therefore, she would find herself in an almost impossible situation.

Today a woman is not dependent upon a man in that same way. She does not have to have a man support her. Most women are quite capable of fending for themselves, and there are worlds of opportunity open to them. They are not victimized by divorce in the way that women were in the New Testament period. Thus one factor, at least, that was behind Jesus' prohibition of divorce does not play a part in the present scene. God's purposes for a permanent union between a man and a woman are not altered. Yet the ill effects of the failure to achieve a permanent union are reduced in our day.

This cultural change, of course, does not affect the ideal of permanent union. Neither does it suggest that the failure to achieve that ideal is unimportant. It does mean, however, that when a real union is not achieved and a couple resort to divorce, the economic consequences of that failure are not so damaging. It increases the possibility that divorce may be the best possible solution to a tragic situation.

We have called divorce either a failure in marriage or an official recognition of failure. We have acknowledged that the divorced person has fallen short of the Christian ideal. It is helpful for us to consider now how Jesus dealt with people who failed.

Although we have no record of Jesus' dealing with a divorced person, we do have many examples of his working with people who had failed in other ways: with a rich young man (Mark 10:17-22), with Nicodemus (John 3:1-15), with the woman of Samaria (John 4:1-22), with Zacchaeus (Luke 19:1-10), and so on. In every instance he dealt with them redemptively. He did not condone their past failure, nor even suggest that they were really not at fault. Neither did he condemn them, denounce them for their failure, nor close the door to their relationship to him or to other people. He took them as they were, helped them to overcome their past, and set them on the way to becoming the kind of persons they were capable of being.

Who can doubt that he would deal in the same way with divorced persons? He would not pretend that your marriage did not fail, nor would he overlook the continuing effects of that failure upon you. He would be concerned about how you handle the crisis. He would help you rebuild your life in the most positive, creative, constructive way. He does not seem to be interested in saying, "You shouldn't have done that." Rather he seems to be interested in saying, "This is the way for you to find the solution to your problems."

Although marriage is one of the most important aspects of life, other things matter, too. Sometimes greater harm is done by a married couple remaining together than by their terminating their marriage. The answer to the question of whether your divorce was right (in a religious sense) must be based upon a consideration of the conflict of values. In some situations the "right" thing (in terms of achieving the ideal) is no longer an option to you. You have to choose between two courses of action, both of which are wrong. In such circumstances you have to do the best possible.

Was divorce the best possible action for you? You cannot respond affirmatively to this question if more people were damaged more severely by your divorce than would have been the case if you had remained together. Just as marriage is not a purely private matter, neither is divorce. You and your former spouse are involved. Your parents are involved. Your children are involved. To a lesser extent, your friends are involved. It hardly seems right to sacrifice everyone else to your own happiness. The question, therefore, is not whether *you* are better off because of your divorce, but whether *everyone involved* is better off.

Neither can you confidently say that divorce was the best possible alternative for you if you did not try in every way to salvage your marriage. Divorce may be right as a last resort; it is improper as the first attempt to deal with marital problems. You are not likely to feel that your divorce was justified unless you leaned over backwards to make your marriage work. Neither are you likely to feel right about it unless you tried to get help in working out your problems. In other words, you may be sure that yours was the right course of action only if you failed in spite of sincere and persistent attempts to make your marriage work.

If you continue to be unforgiving in your attitude toward your partner, you are not likely to feel right about your divorce. This does not mean that you have to accept total responsibility for the failure of your marriage. Neither does it mean that you should hold on to some nope that even yet you might possibly make a go of it. It only means that you cannot nourish that hatred or contempt or resentment which in all probability you felt. A divorce based upon an unwillingness to forgive, even in the case of something as serious as adultery, is not in keeping with Christian character. An unforgiving attitude will haunt you no matter what happens.

What sort of things might indicate that divorce was the best possible solution in your situation? One of them is the cold, hard fact that you might have married someone with whom you could not possibly have a good marriage. At the time of your wedding you may have made a great mistake. Had you been willing to listen to advice from more objective persons you might have avoided it. But you married, and only after your marriage did you begin to see what you could not see before. If there are deep and irreconcilable differences of culture or ideals or attitudes or values or life-styles, there can be no real union of two lives. Although predictions about failure or success can never be made with 100 percent accuracy, in many cases the prospects for failure seem quite clear. If this was true of your situation, then divorce may have been the best course for you to take.

Not all divorces are caused by factors that existed before marriage, however. Sometimes marriages which are successful for a time begin to disintegrate. Something happens to one person or the other—or to both—that drives the couple apart. Success is turned into failure. Attitudes develop, character is altered, personality changes. Two people who had been good for each other may begin to bring out the worst in each other. Recognizing that all other alternatives should have been explored before you resorted to separation, the situation may have reached the point where divorce was the best alternative.

Sometimes, rather than helping an individual become a whole and mature person, marriage destroys that person. This may be the case where one person physically abuses another. If such abuse becomes a pattern, and if it becomes increasingly severe, as is sometimes the case, then divorce may become necessary to protect health and/or life.

More difficult to define, though no less damaging to the person, is psychic abuse. I am not talking about those easy and inane things that sometimes are called "mental cruelty." I am talking about those situations which are *in fact* mental cruelty. One person can destroy another without leaving a mark on the body. In a good marriage husband and wife support each other—help each other to a whole and healthy life. But some husbands and wives tear each other down, crush and destroy each other. If that was happening to you, and again if you had explored all other possibilities, then divorce may have been the best possible course open to you.

Destruction may be the result of a disintegrating marriage even when there is no malicious intent. Two fine and well-intentioned persons may do this to one another. Mary McDermott Shideler tells of a Christian couple who, in the dozen years of their marriage

had separated twice—at least once for more than a year—in order to obtain for themselves and give each other the kind of breathing space they needed in their search for a way to solve their problems without violence. Each thoroughly liked and respected the other. They continued to share many interests. But now their relationship had become destructive of their individual selves and therefore of their union. The details do not matter. Here was simply the not uncommon situation where, in order to grow or even endure, each needed something that the other could not give without destroying his or her very identity as a person, and each was compelled to express in his or her own life something essential which undercut the other's well-being.[4]

In this case neither the man nor the woman could make a case for "mental cruelty." Yet they were destroying each other, and divorce seemed the best thing for them.

If you have children, what was happening to them should have been a consideration in your decision about what to do. It is certainly too glib to say, "It is always better for parents to divorce than for children to be brought up in an unhappy home." Though that is sometimes the case, it is not always so. Sometimes a poor father or mother is better than none. The disadvantages to your children of their being brought up in your own unhappy marriage situation should have been weighed against the disadvantages of their being separated from one or the other of you. The best thing for the children, of course, would be for them to be brought up in a happy home where their parents love and respect each other. That alternative not being open, the scars of separation from one or the other of you may be less than the scars of living with two parents whose hostility destroys everyone in sight.

Resources

There is a common feeling that a divorced person really has no religious resources for helping him deal with this crisis. In a sense, that feeling is valid. If your husband (wife) had died, your church would have offered you all kinds of help. There would have been a memorial service that would have helped you affirm your faith. Your pastor would have visited you. Your friends would have rallied around you. Your church would have prayed with you and for you. You would have had ample opportunity to express your confused and conflicting emotions.

But your husband (wife) whom you have lost is still alive. Your church has no rituals to help you adjust your thinking and your emotions to this strange situation. Your pastor may not know whether to visit you. If he does, he has no religious framework for giving you spiritual aid and comfort. You almost expect him to rebuke you. Your friends don't know whether to express congratulations or sympathy. Your fellow Christians hardly know whether to pray for your forgiveness, to praise God for your deliverance, or to pretend that nothing has really changed.

As a matter of fact, however, there are indeed important spiritual resources available to you. You can begin with the assurance of God's presence with you. He never leaves his children alone, whatever the circumstances of their life. They can cry out to him in the extremes of great joy and great distress. Paul went through a long list of problems and declared that absolutely nothing "will be able to separate us from the love of God in Christ Jesus our Lord" (Rom. 8:39). He even said that "in everything God works for good with those who love him, who are called according to his purpose (Rom. 8:28). Even though he did not include the crisis of divorce in his list of perils, he gave a ringing affirmation of his confidence in the grace of God. That grace is available to you in this crisis.

If you will let him, your pastor can be of great help to you. He is not concerned with condemnation but with healing of the spirit. Whether he approves or diapproves of your divorce is not a basic consideration. What matters is that you can talk things out with him and in that process come to a better understanding of yourself, of what has happened to you, and of what your resources are. He can help you understand what you can do and what you need to do. He can pray for you and with you. If he is a trained counselor, that is an advantage. Whether he is or not, however, he is God's servant to minister to your emotional and spiritual needs.

In this context, you can count upon the fellowship of your church more fully than you realize. The church is not in the business of purging itself of people who fall short of the ideal. If it were seriously to try to do that, hardly anyone would be left. The church is not made up of morally perfect people. It is made up of people who acknowledge that they are sinners. It is made up of people who "bear one another's burdens." It is made up of people who try to help one another fulfill their calling to discipleship. It may not have a well-structured program for helping you in this particular crisis. It has people, however, who take seriously that central element in the Christian life: love.

Notes

1. *Cf.* David Mace, *Hebrew Marriage*, pp. 241-259, for a good discussion of "The Dissolution of Marriage."

2. Clyde Lee Herring, "Dilemma: The Church and Divorce," *People*, June, 1972, p. 33.

3. Shirley Stephens, "A Place for Us," *People*, June, 1972, pp. 26-30.

4. Mary McDermott Shideler, "An Amicable Divorce," *The Christian Century*, May 5, 1971, p. 553.

5. YOUR SOCIAL ADJUSTMENT

The popular picture of the gay divorcee is a fiction. Most divorced persons are not happy and carefree. Their social life is not a whirl of activity. Of all the ways in which you have to start a new life, none will be more difficult than that of working out your relationships with family and friends. The difficulty is tied in with the feeling of loneliness which we discussed in chapter 3. Coleridge's lines describe it vividly:

> Alone, alone, all, all alone,
> Alone on a wide, wide sea!
> And never a saint took pity on
> My soul in agony.

The problem, however, is not simply your feelings. You are in fact in a situation that is new and strange to you. You have never before been divorced. You don't know how to act as a divorcee. Should you go about your "business as usual"? Should you pretend to yourself that nothing important is gone from your life? At work, should you try to be casual about what has happened? How should you act in your community? with your neighbors? in your relationships with other members of your family? Should you start dating?

Self-understanding

If you are to make a successful social adjustment, you will have to come to grips with yourself. What kind of person are you anyway? What do you really like? What do you want to be and to do? What are your hopes and fears? your frustrations? Are you willing to reveal yourself to the whole world? to any one person? To what extent are you being yourself, and. to what extent are you merely fitting into roles assigned to you?

Morton M. Hunt says:

The formerly married person is not who he was; he is another person— but who? The process of convalescence requires a redefinition of his identity, the acquisition of a new sense of who and what he now is. This means the working out of a number of new roles toward people around him.[1]

Writing to the divorced mother, Carol Mindey said:

Your new aloneness will provide you a chance to learn who you really are and who you can become. There is no one to stop you now but yourself. Do you have the courage to find out, to take the risk? Your children cannot fill every void and gap—it would be unfair to expect of them what only another adult can give. But they will keep you busy and may even provide you a purpose for living, until you discover that *you* are the purpose.[2]

Perhaps you have not had much time to think about yourself during the past months, or even the past years. Perhaps you have not had the inclination to do so. Every mature person needs to know himself, however, and your present situation both makes that need more imperative and gives you the opportunity to do something about it.

Recently a student sat in my office crying: "I'm tired of people telling me who I am. I want to find out for myself." That student voiced a concern that is particularly important to you right now. Like most other people, you probably have permitted your life to be determined by the roles into which you have been expected to fit. Now one of those basic roles—that of husband or wife—has suddenly been removed. Another basic role—that of parent—may also have been removed or seriously altered. The new role of divorcee is not as clearly defined. Your adjustment to this new situation will force you to take a long, hard look at yourself.

Certain traditional guidelines to self-discovery may offer you some help in answering the question, Who am I? In theological terms, you are both a child of God and a sinner. Created in God's image, you can commune with him. You are aware of his presence and you can be sure that he is aware of you. You are the crown of creation, given dominion over the rest of creation. You are "a little lower than God." Yet you are also a sinner. By your own choice you have separated yourself from him. You have corrupted your nature and have abused the creation for which you are responsible. As a Christian, you have been brought back to him by his gracious self-giving in Christ. You have ideals for which you strive even though you fall short. You live out your life always aware of his grace which both sustains you and restores you when you fail. You remain an object of his love.

In social terms, you are the product of your environment. You are shaped and formed by your family, your peers, your culture. The roles that you play in your society help you to know what is expected of you. By fitting into those roles, you find life to be secure and comfortable.

Although it is helpful for you to see yourself in these general theological and social terms, however, you share these things with all people. These generalizations help you see yourself in your common humanity; they do not help you see yourself in your individuality. While it is important to understand these things about yourself, it is even more important that you understand yourself as a unique person.

I suggest that you do not so much *discover* who you are as you *decide* who you are. "Discovery" implies that somewhere deep down on the inside there is a real you that is hidden from everyone else and that apparently is hidden even from you. If you go deep enough, however, if you abandon all the roles you play, if you eliminate all those things that other people expect of you, then perhaps the real you can come forth.

"Decision," on the other hand, emphasizes the quality of self-determination. It implies that who you are is fundamentally a matter of your own choice and your own action. Obviously there are certain inherent physical characteristics that are beyond your control. Obviously you cannot ignore your past experiences, for your past has brought you to this present situation. In this present situation, however, you are still making decisions. You are choosing goals. You are selecting companions. You are cultivating this attitude and rejecting that one.

You make decisions partly in terms of your relationships. To relate to a person or an event is to act and to react in a given way. You are deciding who you are when you laugh or cry or become angry. You are deciding who you are when you worship and when you work. You are deciding who you are when you read this book and when you read the morning newspaper and when you watch television. Your relationships with persons and your reaction to things become a part of you.

One of the most important factors by which you determine who you are is your relationship to your family and your friends. By their influence they help to make you what you are. When you decide that you like this person or dislike that one you are deciding what kind of person you want to be. You tend to act like the people you admire. While you cannot choose your family, you can choose your friends. And in choosing, you are deciding who you are.

Perhaps almost as important as the individuals who are your

"inner circle" are the groups that are made up of those individuals. That is to say, your family as a whole influences you in a way that is over and above the influence of all the individuals within your family. The same is true of "the crowd" that is made up of your friends. The group has an identity of its own that makes its mark on you. Your school, your church, your business, your club, your informal group of friends all affect you. As you identify yourself with a group, you help determine who you are.

You cannot control your family or your friends. They make their own decisions. Through their decisions and actions, however, or through those forces of nature over which you exercise no control, situations develop in which you are forced to act. Your response to those situations helps to shape your character.

Although these persons do not control your life, they do create the situation in which you must live. You determine, in large measure, how you respond to them. You determine, therefore, what kind of person you are. It isn't correct to say, "I can't help it; this is the way I feel"—or "think" or "act." Perhaps in the immediate situation you cannot control your emotions or your thoughts. By the choices you make, however, you determine what you shall be feeling or thinking or doing for a long time to come. Within the limitations established by factors beyond your control, you have great freedom. How you use that freedom does not merely show what you are; it helps make you what you are.

To be what many writers call an "authentic person" you need to begin to define yourself in larger terms. You need not—and should not—cut yourself off from those persons who mean a great deal to you—your family and your friends. You will become more authentic, however, if you extend your meaningful relationships as Jesus did. The Gospels make it clear that Jesus' family and friends meant a great deal to him. Yet he once said, "Whoever does the will of God is my brother, and sister, and mother" (Mark 3:35). If you extend your concerns through your work, through your church, through activity in behalf of other people in your community, you will be defining yourself in a way that has much greater meaning.

Work, church, friends, the needs of society, and so on, however, are changeable. What is central to an authentic personhood is a meaningful relationship to Christ himself. He provides an unvariable, a fixed point of reference, that shows fully and completely what it means to be human. Whatever else he has done for us, he has revealed what it means to live to the fullest as a human being. He demonstrated the depths of friendship. He loved all sorts of people: Zacchaeus the publican; Mary Magdalene the prostitute; Nicodemus the Pharisee; the unnamed Gadarene demoniac; and multitudes of the lame, the halt, and the blind. He accepted people as they were. This is what it really means to be human.

You and Your Family

A permanent tie exists between parents and children. Thomas Wolfe wrote that "You can't go home again." As a matter of fact, however, "You can't leave home." Your parents never cease to be parents, and you never cease to be son or daughter. Before you married, your relationship at home may have been either good or bad—or, more probably, a little of both. Your parents may have opposed your marriage or they may have approved of it. You may have kept in close touch with them or you may have contacted them only infrequently. No matter what, however, they are still your parents and you are still their child. Consequently they are affected by your divorce.

Your parents may be upset by your divorce. Parents want to see their children succeed in life. They want them to be secure, to have a good marriage, to rear children in a happy home. Your failure to achieve this ideal may have hurt them. This is especially the case if they believe that divorce is wrong. To their friends they may speak with regret or even a sense of shame about your divorce. Their disapproval may come through to you and may make your own problems even more severe. If they do come through this way, don't be either surprised or angry. It is because they love you that they feel as they do.

Your parents' distress over your divorce may reveal a bit of self-centeredness. They may feel that your failure reflects on them. This is especially true if they cherish the tradition that "There has never been a divorce in our family." The fact that they feel this way, however, should create no barrier between you. In times of distress we all have some feelings and thoughts that are less than noble. Though your parents' distress may have an element of the selfish in it, that is not the whole story. Basically they are concerned for you.

On the other hand, your parents may be relieved by your divorce. They may have been deeply disturbed by what your marriage was doing to you. They may even go to great lengths to tell you how badly you were mistreated and how well off you are now that your marriage is over. They may be convinced that you married the wrong person, that he (she) was not good for you, and that the divorce was his (her) fault. This reaction, too, will be an expression of their love.

In either event, you can surely count upon the love and support of your parents. Just as they soothed your hurts when you were a little child, and just as they were a stabilizing force for you when you were an adolescent, now they will come through again. They will offer you their love. They may be of financial assistance. They may help in the care of your children. They may even invite you to come back home.

Going back home, however, could present problems. In the

months ahead you may have a variety of difficulties—emotional and financial and practical and social. You may have to accept help from your parents or even to ask for it if it is not offered. If so, you will be better off if you take that help only on a temporary basis. As an adult, you must accept full responsibility for your own actions. This means not only the responsibility for the failure of your marriage; it means also your new responsibilities in your status as a divorced person and perhaps in the status of a parent without a partner.

Emotionally you cannot return to the status of a child in the home of your parents. You are accustomed to a kind of self-determination that you never had when you lived with your parents. No matter how much freedom they gave you, you were not to them just another young person. You were their son or daughter. They cared where you were, who your friends were, what you did, when you came in at night, and so on. It will be hard for them not to have the same concerns if you go back home. Furthermore, you may find yourself tending to slip back into that role in spite of yourself. You will see yourself in the old relationship of dependence.

Temporary help from your parents, in other words, may be necessary. A long-range dependence will be disastrous.

If it is at all possible, you should keep on good terms with your former in-laws. It may be easy to do so, particularly if they do not blame you for the breakup of your marriage. It may be hard to do so, however, if they side with your former partner. In either case, they are the grandparents of your children. Your children may love them and want to keep in touch with them. Even if they do not, or if they are too young to remember very long, your former in-laws may need it. The jokes about the proud, doting grandparents are based on a fact of life. Grandparents take pride in how cute and how smart their grandchildren are. That pride does not suddenly cease when the parents of those grandchildren separate. Give your children the privilege of enjoying the love of all their grandparents. And do not deprive grandparents of their delight in their grandchildren even if you can no longer live with your husband (wife).

To the Parents of a Divorcee

If perchance a father or a mother of a divorced person is reading this book, you are urged to take note of three simple recommendations. First, please don't say to your son or daughter, "I told you so." If you opposed the marriage to begin with, you don't need to say so now. Your son or daughter already knows that and does not want to be reminded now. Facing the fact of failure, nothing will be less helpful than the reminder that you were right all the time.

Second, offer all the help that you can in the immediate crisis. Your son or daughter may need money. He may need a place to stay. He may need help in working out plans for the care of children. He may need someone to listen to him pouring out all the pent-up emotions and hostilities and fears. He certainly will need the reassurance that no matter what has happened, and no matter who was at fault, your love does not end.

And third, don't expect your son or daughter to return to you the same person as before. He is not simply a single person, the son or daughter that you gave up some years ago; he is a formerly married person. A lot has happened to change him. Such would have been the case simply by virtue of the passing time, even apart from marriage. But all of this time he has had the responsibilities of a married person, perhaps of parenthood, certainly of maintaining a home, of keeping up with job responsibilities. He cannot and should not any longer be regarded as the child he once was. He needs your help and you need to give it. Give the help that is needed, however, without trying to make him revert to childhood. Let him be independent. Respect him as a mature person who is trying to deal with his own problems.

You and Your Friends

One of the most baffling situations you will face is that of relationships with friends. Before your divorce, your social activities involved you as a married person. In general, single people have single friends and married people have married friends. After you married, in all probability you gradually moved into a new social circle of married people. Not only did you "party" together, but your whole social contact was with them. You lived either in an apartment building with other couples, or in a house in a community of married people. At church you were grouped with people like you in age, sex, *and marital status.* The same is true of your civic or social clubs.

With whom will you associate now? Your friends will have some very practical problems at this point. Suppose, for example, that a group of you used to get together once in a while for bridge. Now which of you stays with the group? And if it is you, who is your bridge partner? Suppose someone has a party; which of you is to be invited? Suppose you were in a "couples class" in Sunday School; do both of you continue to attend?

Your married friends may have to choose up sides between you. It will be difficult for them, at any rate, not to side with one or the other of you. It will be equally difficult for the men to continue their friendship with the divorced man and the women with the divorced woman. That might even lead to some conflict in their own marriage. It may become necessary for them to side with one or the other of you. Not wanting to become involved, however, they may simply drop both of you.

The upshot of it all is that you are likely to have to make some new friends. If you move to another town, of course, that will be necessary anyway. If you remain in the same town, however, you may begin to feel a bit uncomfortable with people who have been friends of both of you.

As you move into a new social setting you will be adjusting to a new status. You are neither single nor married. You are divorced. Protest all you like that you are an individual, with unique characteristics, in a unique situation, with unique personality, and so on. It is all in vain, for society assumes certain things about us in terms of the roles in which we are cast. The role of a divorced person is different from that of both married persons and single persons. You will be treated as a divorcee. That treatment will make it hard for you to be yourself.

All of this is not to suggest that you stand alone. You have friends and they will stand by you. They may not understand the turmoil that you are experiencing, and they may not always know when they are most needed or what you want or expect of them. You may have to tell them frankly and openly. If they are true friends, however, they will be there when you need them. Carol Mindey wrote of her experience:

Without friends, those six years would have been almost unbearable. I've had no relatives at hand to count on; I didn't have the kind of neighbors who come in and pitch in when one is rushed to the hospital or is sick; but I've had the most loyal and best friends I could ever hope for.[3]

Do not be upset by the initial attitudes of people whom you meet. When we are trying to get acquainted with new people we start with certain categories. Marital status is one of the most important ones. Not all single men and women are alike; not all married people are alike; and not all divorced people are alike. Yet we reach certain conclusions about people on the basis of what we know about others in the same category. Beyond that, there is a kind of role expectation which almost lends itself to the idea, "I know all about you; you are divorced." If you will remember two things, however, you can avoid being hurt by this kind of prejudice. First, divorced people are not singled out for this kind of treatment. All people experience the same thing. And second, this role-assignment is the beginning of getting acquainted, not the end. In due season you will not be regarded as a divorcee but as a person.

Sooner or later you are likely to face the question of dating. What you decide will be influenced by many factors, one of the most important of which will be your attitude toward the possibility of remarriage. This possibility will be examined in a later chapter. Here, however, we must consider the question of dating because it is the basic pattern of social relationships between unmarried people.

Let us begin with the recognition that nearly all persons both want and need companionship of persons of the opposite sex. Though sexual intercourse is the most intimate and the ultimate expression of the sex drive, it is far from the only form of expression. The male-female relationship gets involved in our work and our play, in our politics and in our religion, in our education and in our community life. We never stop being a man or a woman. It is important that we understand that the one is incomplete without the other.

Furthermore, we are culturally conditioned to think of ourselves in terms of male or female in relationship to each other. We are not impervious to the influence of the people around us. We see people paired off all the time, not only in the movies and in TV but also in real life. Whether deliberately or subconsciously, our friends tend to match us up with some eligible person. Surrounded by people who have paired off with one another, we almost feel left out if we do not follow the same pattern.

Every society has its own method of matching people up. In most places in the world and for most of the world's history, it has been the responsibility of parents to find prospective mates for their children. In our society, however, since the colonial period, the young people themselves have had a good deal to say about it. For the past fifty years they have virtually taken the entire responsibility upon themselves. Young people find one another at the school, at a party, in the neighborhood, on the job. This system has its faults, but it has worked fairly well.

One of the faults of the system is the matter that concerns you right now. The system does not know what to do with and for divorced persons. In the past there were relatively few such persons around and the pressure for taking care of them did not exist. Now that divorce is becoming so common, however, more and more people find themselves frustrated in the effort to find a meaningful and satisfactory social life.

Whatever patterns emerge, one fact stands out: If you are going to meet persons whom you might be interested in dating, you have to go where those persons are. You may find them at work or at church or at parties. Mutual friends may arrange for you to meet. You might find them in your own neighborhood. You might find them in community activities. In such situations you are not necessarily in the market for another marriage partner. You are simply recognizing that you need friendship and companionship.

In all such social contacts, another consideration is important. Even though you are making no commitment more serious than a tentative social arrangement, the kind of person you associate with is perhaps even more important now than before you married. Like it or not, you are probably being watched more closely and by more people. Your reputation is more at stake. Furthermore, if you should become seriously involved with anyone, it should be someone with whom the prospects for a successful marriage are good. You need to associate with people whose convictions and ideals and aspirations are the same as yours. If you date, there is always the possibility that you may become serious and want to marry. If you fall in love again, you need to be very careful about the kind of person you fall in love with.

The Sexual Adjustment

Another extremely difficult adjustment you will have to make is in the area of sex. The sex drive knows nothing about marital status. Single, married, widowed, divorced—we all are sexual beings. We are responsive not just to the person to whom we are married but to many people. In a given set of circumstances, and without any necessary intent to evoke a response on the part of either person, almost any normal male and any normal female might be sexually responsive to each other. As one person frankly put it, "My mouth waters whenever I see a beautiful apple, regardless of whether that apple is mine." You will not lose all sex desire simply because you are no longer married.

Most married couples, whether they are happy or not, develop a pattern of sex expression. That relationship may not be entirely satisfactory, as for many it is not. Or, on the other hand, it may be almost the only thing that holds a couple together. In either event it is a pattern of expression. Even a couple whose marriage has deteriorated to the point that they resort to divorce is likely to have come together sexually fairly frequently right up to the time of their separation.

This pattern of sexual expression is extremely difficult to

terminate. Initially you may feel vastly relieved to be free of the obligation. It will not be long, however, before you begin to miss the intimacy of lovemaking. Bereaved persons experience the same thing. One woman, widowed at the age of thirty after ten years of marriage, wrote:

One month after my husband's death I had my 30th birthday. By then I had discovered that no one around me was able to broach the delicate subject of sex. The initial shock pumps adrenalin into your body to carry you through the burial, and after that you feel physically drained. But then—the time lapse depends on the individual—a feeling of irritability pervades you. The fact that you miss the touch, the warmth and the lovemaking is a positive statement about your marriage, not a negative statement about you. . . . I felt no guilt when my body throbbed at 3 A.M. as I lay there in a half-empty bed.[4]

Students of the family generally agree that most divorced persons do not for long abstain from sexual intercourse. Morton M. Hunt says:

Of all the people one might meet in the World of the Formerly Married at any given moment, almost none of the men and only about one-fifth of the women have had no sexual intercourse at all since their marriages broke up. Obviously time plays a part in this: the longer a person remains an FM, the greater the likelihood that he or she will have begun having postmarital sexual activity. But most people start very soon; five out of six FM's begin having sexual intercourse within the first year, most of them with more than one partner.[5]

Although Hunt's statement is bluntly put, most writers agree with him.

We are not concerned about averages, however. We are concerned about you and your decisions. Whatever the majority of people do, you make your own decision. There seem to be three alternatives open to you. First, you may seek satisfaction for your sexual desire without serious consideration as to who your partner is. Many formerly married persons, when sexual desire is strong, simply find a congenial companion for the moment. There is no hint of any mutual commitment and no concern beyond a pleasurable experience. Such encounters, however, are more likely to occur in the earlier weeks or months of separation. For many people they are really expressions of self-doubt: are they capable of giving pleasure to someone else? For others it is a declaration of freedom: there are no strings attached. For still others it is almost like getting drunk: it is a means of forgetting. Hunt aptly designates people who have this kind of experience "users" and says of them:

Most formerly married people are either fearful or actually incapable of loving again soon after the disintegration of their marriages, but are unwilling to do without sex until love comes along; yet it is not just that they are unwilling to abstain—they need sex for urgent reasons, and use it as a means of gaining important goals.[6]

It should be observed that to use sex in this way is to abuse it. It is to fail to see that sex is not merely a biological function. Worse still, it is to fail to see that persons are damaged by the impersonality of such a relationship.

A second alternative is to enter into temporary liaisons. Many formerly married people pair off for a time without any idea of a permanent commitment. So long as they find their total relationship—including sexual intercourse—to be mutually satisfying the relationship continues. They are not entirely casual about it, for they recognize that sex is an intensely personal matter and that sexual intercourse is tied in with all other aspects of their relationship. It is one aspect of their pleasure in being together. They speak no words of love. They make no demands upon each other and no promises to each other. They both understand that the relationship is not permanent.

From a Christian perspective this kind of relationship is better than promiscuity. Yet, it too is seriously deficient. We all long for permanence and security and exclusiveness in our personal relationships. Without intending to do so, Hunt brings out this point in his description of one such liaison:

And when they part on Monday morning he will be vague about when they are to meet again, for after each spell of intimacy he becomes uneasy and elusive for a while. He has made it clear that he dates other women. She realizes that having only recently gotten his "freedom" after a long divorce fight, he needs to feel unfettered, and she is baffled and frustrated by his doing with her so many things both tender and fierce, trivial and important, which she always took to mean love, and which now seems to mean much less. Once in a while she cries a little, silently, after they make love; if he notices, he says nothing, for what good could come of it?[7]

A third alternative is continence, and it is this alternative which is most appropriate for the Christian. It is not an easy ideal. Doubtless you did not find it easy before you were married. For reasons already stated, you are not likely to find it easier now. The sex drive is a powerful force. You live in a culture that is highly charged with sexual stimuli. You may find yourself attracted to many persons. There may seem many reasons why continence is unnecessary. Only a genuine commitment to the belief that it is the right thing will be an adequate reason for continence.

In spite of what you may read, and in spite of what you may be told, continence is in no sense abnormal and in no sense unhealthy. A rejection of your sexual nature, a denial that you have a sex drive, is abnormal and unhealthy. But a recognition of that drive and a deliberate, rational decision to abstain is both desirable and possible.

The reason for thinking that abstinence is right and proper is not merely the prohibitions that are found in the Bible, though they should not be minimized. In the experience of most people, sex without commitment is fundamentally unsatisfactory. Whether it is a one-night stand or a liaison that lasts for months, any relationship that is known to be casual and temporary is deprived of an essential quality. However casual a person may appear about sex, most people learn that it is not an end in itself but that it is central and fundamental in a total man-woman relationship. To be fundamentally satisfying sexual intercourse demands love, acceptance, and commitment.

A failure to understand this nature of the sex relationship may have been involved in the disintegration of your marriage. If, so, you will not solve any basic problem now by a further abuse of sex.

How are you, then, to deal with your sex drive if you choose continence? Unsatisfied, the sexual urge at times may make you restless, irritable, upset.

Kinsey found that a large percentage of formerly married persons resorted to masturbation for release of tensions. Some authorities recommend this as a helpful procedure. Dr. Mary S. Calderone, for example, says:

Far better to have self-release than to indulge in a temporary and therefore shabby relationship. . . . From the standpoints both of [the formerly-married person's] emotional well-being and his social adjustments, I submit that . . . self-release fulfills a necessary function.[8]

From the point of view of many Christians, masturbation is sinful. The Roman Catholic Church teaches that such is the case and so do many individual Protestant Christians. The biblical basis for this view is the story of Onan (Gen. 38:1-11). The point of that story, however, is something entirely different, and nowhere else does the Bible deal with the issue. Perhaps the most that can be said is that masturbation is characteristic of immaturity. The vast majority of adolescents, both boys and girls, practice it at times. They find it one way of relieving the sexual stresses and tensions in this most difficult and stormy period of life. The adult who resorts to it, therefore, is resorting to a pre-adult form of release.

Many people sublimate the sex drive by finding some demanding form of physical activity which drains them of their energy. Working or playing to the point of exhaustion is hardly the same as sexual intercourse. It may, however, be the means by which you defuse the explosive desire. Some people who are permanently unmarried—either never-married, or widowed, or divorced—find that self-giving either to their work or to avocational pursuits is the best way to handle the situation.

Dorothy W. Payne, who has been married, divorced, and widowed, and who now is an ordained minister conducting an experimental ministry to single women, writes of her own experience:

Through the past few years many women have asked me how I overcame my own physical passions. I share with you here some of the devices I used to channel this energy. You may find others. (1) Confession of the struggle. It's important here to find someone you can trust or learn to trust. Trust itself can heal discontent and can discipline and channel energy. (2) Prayer and reflection in the light of the reality of the situation, and a willingness to change. (3) Exercise and deep breathing often help momentarily. Let your mind move to something else as you move about. (4) Reading a book which is not titillating. This, like exercise, is one of the least effective diversions, since it is so temporary. But anything that helps you see you will not die of the pain aids in self-control. (5) Finger painting, water-coloring, rhythmic movements, writing, singing, playing an instrument, are ways of finding yourself in the highest sense. (6) Studying the subject of sex and personhood from an academic standpoint with the purpose of learning how to use this God-given energy.

(7) Learning to deal with other frustrations in your life. (8) Learning more about all forms of love, and disciplining yourself to reach out to others to help and for help. (9) Deepening relationships with a few primary persons in life is the best way I have found. (10) Attempting to use your total love-energy to serve God and your neighbor.[9]

Whatever techniques you discover, there is no substitute for rational decision and commitment. If you decide that for you continence is to be the way, then you can make it so. If your religious conviction determines that sexual intercourse is properly a marital relationship only, then it can be so. You do not have to deny the fact that you are sexually responsive. Indeed, your emotional and spiritual health demands that you recognize the fact. But if you understand what sex is in the relationship of a man and a woman committed to each other under God, if you regard it as potentially beautiful and mean-ingful in marriage but empty and meaningless outside marriage, then you have provided for yourself an adequate framework for dealing with the drive. For you, continence will be not the way of frustration and emotional disorder, but the way of stability and strength and security.

Do not misunderstand. Many people do not fuse sex and love. Some people have pleasurable sexual experiences outside marriage and are not necessarily plagued by a sense of guilt. Neither do they believe that their practices will interfere with their eventually entering into a happy and successful marriage.

The fact that some people do not find such extramarital experiences disastrous, however, does not alter the situation for you. As a Christian you are concerned not only with personal happiness but also with living as fully as possible in harmony with the spirit of Christ. No one—single, married, or divorced— can live a life that is free of all frustrations and difficulties. The richest life—and the one with the greatest potential for dealing with every situation in life—is the one that holds to the highest ideals. For an unmarried person, the ideal of continence is a high and difficult one. But it is, in my judgment, the one that holds the greatest promise.

Notes

1. Morton M. Hunt, *The World of the Formerly Married* (New York: McGraw-Hill, 1966), p. 63.

2. Mindey, *op. cit.*, p. 152.

3. *Ibid.*, p. 163.

4. Joyce A. Phipps, "What Really Happens When Your Husband Dies?" *Christian Century*, February 21, 1973, p. 231.

5. Hunt, *op. cit.*, p. 144.

6. *Ibid.*, p. 153.

7. *Ibid.*

8. Quoted in Hunt, *op. cit.*, p. 150.

9. Dorothy W. Payne, *Women Without Men* (Philadelphia: Pilgrim Press, 1969), pp. 54-55.

6. YOUR CHILDREN

A child does not have to be traumatized by the divorce of his parents.

Many children are, to be sure. For a variety of reasons, none of which we need go into here, many children are incapable of handling the situation which led their parents to terminate their marriage.

On the other hand, after their parents have separated, many children have adjusted quite well to their new family situation. One child psychiatrist found that a relatively low percentage of her patients were children of divorced parents. Her observation is that the fact of divorce itself does not often severely disturb a child emotionally. "It is not divorce, but the emotional situation in the home, with or without divorce, that is the determining factor in a child's adjustment. A child is very disturbed when the relationship between his parents is very disturbed." [1]

How well your child is able to adjust to the fact of your divorce is not now entirely in your hands. All of the past is involved in his reactions. Whether he is with you or your former partner and the way the two of you act, are involved in it. The things that now happen to you and to your former partner will be involved in it.

Yet you will have a great deal to do with your child's adjustment. You can make what is for him a difficult situation even worse. Or you can help him in this period of great change

in his life. Change is always difficult—even when it is obviously
a change for the better. You need to do all you can to make
this change a constructive experience for your child, one from
which he will emerge a stronger and more secure individual.

For Better or for Worse?

There is no point in discussing here the question of whether
your child is better off or worse off because of your divorce.
The divorce is an accomplished fact. The urgent question
becomes now, How can we make sure that life will become
better?

The best environment in which a child can grow up is a
happy home where his parents love each other and together
provide for the needs of their child. Although there may be
conflict in such a home, it is conflict that does not divide.
In such a home there are problems, but they are problems
which the family attack together. The crises which arise, as
they do in all families, in the long run will pull the family
closer together. A shared faith, a common set of values, a
unity of purpose, and a mutual commitment provide security
and challenge to all the members of the family.

That kind of home, however, ceased to be an option in your
case, perhaps long before the separation occurred. Many homes
are characterized by what Despert calls an "emotional divorce."
Often a couple are together (or "married") only in the sense
that they live in the same house. There is a distance between
them characterized either by open conflict or by an armed
truce or by a silent indifference. A legal divorce is almost
always preceded by such an emotional divorce. Yet emotional
divorce does not always result in a legal termination of the
marriage. Children who grow up in homes where both parents

are physically present but emotionally divorced have real trouble in achieving a satisfactory emotional adjustment to life. Growing up in an armed camp is not conducive to inner peace. The presence of two parents does not guarantee partnership in the rearing of children.

What I am saying is that it does your children no good for you to preserve the *form* of marriage and at the same time demonstrate that the *content* of your marriage is dangerous and destructive. What does it do to a child's understanding of maturity and of marriage when he sees his parents either hostile to each other or indifferent to each other? How can they know what mutual respect, affection, and love are when they see no evidence of them at home? How can they be secure when they see that they are the only thing that holds their parents together?

This line of reasoning does not mean that your child is necessarily better off now that you have separated. Divorce is no automatic solution to your personal problems. All that you have done is to make a change which may get everybody concerned out of a bad situation. Whether everyone is now better off is yet to be determined.

This line of reasoning does mean that now there is the possibility for your child to live in a better emotional environment than before. The presence of one parent who has a good relationship with his child may be better for the child than the presence of two parents—even two loving parents—whose bad relationship with each other disrupts the lives of everyone.

Nothing that has been said should be understood to minimize the fact that your divorce probably has upset your child. It is a blow which can shake him terribly, and you must be aware of how he is taking it. All that we are saying here is that now you have both the opportunity and the responsibility to make this situation helpful rather than harmful for him.

Emotional Reactions

Because every individual is different, and because every family situation is different, it is impossible to understand your child's reactions fully in terms of how other children have reacted to the divorce of their parents. Yet there is enough similarity between people and between situations for us to be able to make some helpful generalizations. If you know what reactions have characterized other children in similar situations, then you may be able to deal more effectively with your own child's problems.

Many children are plagued with a feeling of guilt over the separation of their parents. They may have reason for feeling that they are responsible for what has happened. They may have heard their parents argue over their conduct or their disciplines or expenditures for them, for example. They may have overheard once—or many times—one parent shout to another: "If it weren't for the children, I'd leave right now." The inevitable result is that the children will then feel somehow responsible for their parents' unhappiness.

Even if they have not heard such disputes, children may somehow feel guilty. They may feel that they have done something that caused their parents to separate, or that they have failed to do something that would have kept them together. Because of our usual disciplinary methods, children generally associate bad things that happen to them with bad things that they have done. Being separated from one of their parents is "bad." Could it be that their parents separated because of something "bad" they have done?

As an example of the way this feeling of guilt works, Earl Grollman quotes one youngster as crying: "Don't leave, Daddy, I will put away my toys. I promise, honest." Again he cites the case of a little boy who had once said in anger, "I hope

I never see you again." When his parents separated, he felt that his words had made his father leave.[2]

In the face of the fact of separation and divorce, many children employ the defense mechanism of denial. They refuse to accept the fact that a permanent change has taken place. They act as if the separation of their parents is only temporary, and that sooner or later Mother or Daddy will be coming back. Small children often ask for their missing parent or go looking for him in the places where they used to find him. Children who are a little older, and who may understand intellectually what has happened, nevertheless often cling to a hope for a reconciliation. They may even ask from time to time, "When is Daddy coming back home?"

Sometimes children pretend to ignore or to be unaffected emotionally by what has happened. A child may go about his play as if nothing has happened, may make no comment at all about the missing parent, may seem completely unaffected by the change. In such a case, he is probably trying to avoid the pain of the loss or to relieve his anxiety by pretending that his world has not really been upset. If your child acts this way, you should not assume that "He's taking it great." Sooner or later he will have to accept the reality of the situation. You should not add to his pain by cruel or hostile remarks about your former partner. Yet neither should you keep your child in his world of fantasy by lying or by telling half-truths that hold out to him the hope of the return of his missing parent.

A fourth common emotional reaction is regression. Your child may return to some of his more childish ways of behavior. He may start sucking his thumb again, or wetting his bed, or talking baby talk. He may misbehave so as to attract attention. Such regression is likely to be only temporary, however, and is therefore no reason for grave concern on your part.

It is only his way of begging for security and for reassurance of affection. Give him what he needs, and he will soon accept the new situation.

Like adults under stress, your child may become the victim of various forms of bodily distress. He may become restless; he may lose his appetite; he may become physically ill; he may have trouble sleeping, or he may have bad dreams; he may be easily moved to tears or to anger. All of these are matters over which he has no conscious control. He is not so much *acting* as he is *reacting* to a situation in which he perceives himself to be in danger.

One of the most troublesome emotional reactions of your child may be a hostility directed against you. Whatever the circumstances that led to your divorce, your child may blame you for his being deprived of his other parent. By both word and deed he may tell you that he resents you for what you have done. He may want to retaliate by increasing the pain which you already feel. This kind of reaction does not call for punishment, for your child has already had all the trouble he can take. He needs to express his own fears, his own resentment, his own inner pain. Although it is difficult for you, it is essential to his emotional health that you allow him to do so.

At best, your child is likely to be confused. Two people whom he loves and upon whose love he depends no longer love each other. The "ideal family life" is not a possibility now, and he may wonder whether it is ever a possibility for anyone. The values to which his father gives his allegiance are different from those of his mother. Are all men like his father? all women like his mother? all marriages like theirs? The confusion is likely to be compounded if both of you either are or claim to be people of religious faith and conviction. What good is religion if it does not resolve such problems?

Are the two of you hypocrites? Does he have to believe that one of you is Christian and therefore good, and the other not Christian and therefore bad?

If you have noticed a similarity between the emotional reactions of your child, as described here, and the emotional reactions which you yourself experience, it is not by accident. After all, the emotional structure of human beings is essentially the same. Your child's reactions, though at an immature level, often mirror your own. Indeed, it was from you and your former partner that he learned how to act and react!

One fact is fundamental to your dealing helpfully with these emotional responses of your child. In all instances, they are the efforts of your child to adjust to this disruption of his world that has taken place. In time, in all probability, he will get his feet on the ground and will be able to live a normal and happy life. In the meantime you should continue to assure him in every way of your love and concern. Help him face up to the reality of the situation, but do not be harsh and cruel. Allow him to act as a child, while you act as an adult. His actions are cries for help. Give him that help.

You can help make this experience a healing one for your child. You can help him deal with the trauma of separation. You can relieve him of his guilt and fear. You can provide the security which he must have if he is to be emotionally healthy. You can help him accept the weaknesses and failures of the people whom he loves. To do all of this is not easy. It requires all of the strength you can muster. You yourself will have to draw upon your emotional and spiritual resources more than ever before. But you can do it.

If you are to help your child in this way you will have to spend time with him. I am not here talking about that time that you will of necessity spend in caring for his physical needs. Neither am I talking about just being in his presence, at mealtime or watching TV or working while he is playing. I am talking about time devoted to him exclusively, time when you can talk together or do things together. Although it does not have to be a great deal of time, there ought to be a period each day that is devoted to him alone. It should be given priority over other activities and obligations. It should be a time when there are few distractions. If in this way you can strengthen the rapport that is between you, you and your child will then be able to deal together with the extremely difficult situation that your child is in.

Explaining the Divorce

The almost inevitable hostilities between you and your partner before your separation clearly have been a traumatic experience for your child. The present situation is perhaps puzzling and certainly distressing. How can you best make him understand what has happened? There is no simple answer to this question because there are so many variables. It will depend in part upon the age and sex of your child. It will depend in part upon how overt and violent was the hostility which led to your separation. It will depend in part upon the relationship which each of you had to your child prior to the separation. Most difficult of all, it will depend in part upon your child's perception of his role in the breakup of your marriage.

The best way for a child to understand what is happening is for his divorcing parents to prepare him before the fact. It is unnecessary to discuss the problem with him when the matter is only being contemplated, for that would only create fears as to what might take place. If the divorce does not occur, then those fears were created unnecessarily and may leave their mark in terms of a continuing insecurity on the part of the child.

It is the responsibility of both parents to work with a child to help him understand. Together they should say, "We have decided that we do not want to be married to each other any longer." They should choose their words carefully so as not to let the child get the impression that he is in any way responsible. They should not talk with him about it in the heat of their anger against each other, for he might feel that their anger is directed against him. They should tell the truth as they see it, but they do not need to go into details which he cannot understand and which would make no difference to him.

If you and your former partner acted wisely in dealing with your child before your divorce, your task is much easier now. Whether or not you were wise then, however, you now want to help your child understand both intellectually and emotionally what is happening to him and what he might expect in the future.

Do not hold out to your child any false hope that you and his father or mother might get together again. As we indicated in chapter 3, from time to time you may toy with the idea of a possible reconciliation. Most divorced people do. Unless there is a real possibility, however, you should be very careful not to encourage your child to believe that it may happen. If you can honestly say, "We are trying our best to work out a way for us to get back together," it might be well to say so. But if there is no possibility, you should not lie about it. If, even by evasion of your child's questions, you give him any false hope, you are compounding his problem.

Do not make your children choose between the two of you. In some circumstances, of course, a child has to do just that. Or, more correctly, circumstances beyond his control cut him off completely from one of his parents. But you must be very careful not to make your child hate someone whom he loves.

Do not play the role of the innocent victim of the cruelty of his other parent. Admit to yourself, and to your child if need be, your share in the responsibility for the failure of your marriage. Point out to your child, whenever you have the opportunity, the love which your former partner has for him. This may be difficult to do, but the important consideration here is the well-being of your child.

If your divorce was amicable and if you are sufficiently mature, you may be able to concentrate on the positive qualities of the absent parent. Speaking from her own experience, Carol Mindey says:

Children need to identify with both parents, particularly with the parent of their sex. When you are angry with your child, do not say "You're just like your father," because your child may conclude that you hate him the same way you must hate his father. Make positive comparisons, such as "John is an excellent swimmer, like his dad," and your child will be proud of himself and of his father. . . . It hurts a child to think that his parents dislike one another so completely that they can see only the negative qualities in one another.[3]

What has been said thus far assumes that your divorced partner loves his child and wants to maintain as much contact as possible. That is certainly true in most instances. If he (she) does not in fact try to maintain contact, however, should you nevertheless assure your child of his continuing love? Should you make excuses for him in order to keep alive in your child a sense of being loved? Many people say yes. They believe that the worst thing that can happen to a child is a feeling of being rejected. Even if one of his parents does in fact reject him, they say, he should be shielded from that fact if at all possible.

Such deception, however, is really not possible. What can you say about a father who still lives in the vicinity but nevertheless hardly ever sees his child? about a mother who runs off and forsakes her children? Should a child be told that such a father or mother really loves him? Even a very young child would have trouble believing such a thing. Love is communicated by action, not by words alone. If a parent demonstrates by his actions that he does not love his child, the child will know it no matter what anyone says.

This is a way of saying that you should not cover up for a parent who does in fact neglect his child. You should not be cruel in pointing the neglect out to your child. Certainly you should not poison his mind with your reading of what the other person is doing. You should not thwart any effort of his to show his love. But you need not pretend that love is there when in fact it is not.

Your child needs to have as accurate as possible a picture of both of you as you are: your weaknesses and strengths, your faults and virtues, your liabilities and assets. He needs to understand that neither of you is perfect. He needs to love both of you and to be loved by both of you. You can best help him adjust to the fact of your divorce by giving him the opportunity to work things through for himself, at his level of maturity, with honest information.

Visitation Rights

Traditionally the courts have awarded the mother custody of children unless there was some specific reason for doing otherwise. That tradition is changing, however, and increasingly the courts are giving equal consideration to the rights and claims of the father. In a sense this is a real plus, for the decision is then based more upon what is best for the child in each situation.

In most instances, again unless there is reason to do otherwise, the courts grant "reasonable visiting rights" to the parent who does not get custody of the child. Whether such an arrangement is really in the best interest of the child is not at all certain. It often results in each parent trying to alienate the child from the other. In such case, the child is the innocent victim of a continuing battle between his parents. Yet it does seem needlessly cruel not only to the child but also to the parent to cut off all contact even though visits are quite possible.

Since visitation rights usually are granted, however, and since absent parents usually exercise those rights, you should do all within your power to make those visits happy experiences for your child. If you have custody, your former mate probably has worked out plans for having the child at regular intervals. As the two of you implement these arrangements, your paramount concern cannot be your own happiness but the welfare of your child. The two of you will therefore have to cooperate much more closely than apparently was possible for you as husband and wife.

You should make every effort not to spoil the occasion for your child or for his other parent. Issue no warnings—to your child or to his father (mother). Lay down no ultimatum. Cooperate with their plans. Have your child ready on time. If his father (mother) is late arriving, make no snide remarks. Give to your child no hint of your resentment at what is happening. Since you and your former partner are mature adults, you can at least be polite and considerate. In so doing you will ease things for your child.

Your child probably will appreciate it if you can arrange for his other parent to participate in events of special significance to him. Programs at school, birthdays, holidays—these are usually family events. Because of your divorce they cannot be so for your child in the same way as they are for most other children. Yet if they can be so at all your child will be happier.

Carol Mindey sums up this approach quite well:

My sons spend every other weekend with their father. I try to find out what they will be doing so that I can pack the right clothing. If he plans to take them to dinner right after he picks them up, I devote an extra half-hour to helping them select their clothes, and assist them with hair-washing and grooming. This makes my sons know that it is important to me that they have a good visit, and it also shows that I want to be proud of them. I want them to be happy with me when they leave, happy with themselves, and ready to relax and enjoy their dad. Some women may be afraid that their children will like Father better than Mother. If you have this fear, examine it carefully. If you are a loving and concerned mother, you will want your children to love their father. Any love they give to him or to any other human being will certainly not detract from the love they feel for you.[4]

If you do not have custody of your child, but instead have only the right of visiting him from time to time, you are at something of a disadvantage. You live away from him, perhaps in an apartment with no arrangements for children. You have had to rearrange your life—your home routine, your work patterns, your social activities. If you have remarried, your new husband or wife complicates your relationship with your child. If your new mate has children, the problem becomes even more complex. You have to work out your visit with your child in terms of convenience to yourself in your new situation, and your former mate in his (her) situation. With it all you will be trying to make the visit a happy experience for your child.

If you genuinely love your child, you will not try to buy his affection. Because you have little contact with him, you may try to load him down with gifts, or to spend all your time together in "fun and games." You may try desperately to convince him that you are in fact a good and loving parent—

even that he would be better off with you. Although you may not intend it as such, these efforts may be your attempt to win your child away from your former mate. You cannot reverse the court's decision, however. All that you will succeed in doing is to confuse your child and make him even more dissatisfied with his lot in life.

"Fun and games," in fact, is a most abnormal situation. Your child needs not your gifts but you. He needs to learn from you. He needs to be disciplined by you. He needs to be with you at work as well as at play. He needs your counsel and advice. He needs your interest in his activities. He needs your example. He needs, in short, those things which you would supply if you were still living at home with him. Although you cannot supply them in the same way and to the same extent, you may be able to do something. If your child is not better off because of your visits with him, you would do well to forego those visits no matter how much they mean to you.

Your continuing interest in your child should not be confined to those weekly or monthly visits. No matter what has happened between you and your former mate, your child is a part of your life. You have a continuing responsibility to him and for him. You may succeed in separating yourself from an unhappy marriage. You cannot succeed in severing your relationship with your child. His physical well-being is in part your responsibility, no matter what happens. His emotional health and development are in part your responsibility. Perhaps the most painful aspect of your divorce is not being able to be with your child every day and in not being able to play that part in his life which you feel you should play. You will do well, therefore, to make special arrangements for special occasions, to keep in touch by telephone, to anticipate developing needs and provide for them.

All that has been said about visitation rights presumes a

cooperative if not a cordial relationship between you and your former marriage partner. If you do not have that kind of relationship, you are the one who will suffer most. The parent who has custody of the child has the upper hand. One way or another, he calls the shots about when and under what circumstances you can see your child. As we have indicated, your child needs you. Your meeting that need demands that you do everything within your power to get the cooperation of your former partner.

It may develop that your child would be better off if he had only minimal contact with you. If your relationships with your child were stormy before you were divorced, they are not likely to be better now. If you were a poor parent then, your divorce does not make you a better one. A violent temper is not healed by a divorce. Neither is alcoholism or indifference or suspicion or self-centeredness or any of the other things that trouble a family. Occasionally a divorce will bring a person to his senses, make him take stock of himself, and effect a change in his character or personality. More often, however, it only adds failure in marriage to an already long list of personal problems. If that is what has happened in your case, you will do well to consider whether in fact you should exercise your right of visitation!

What I am saying to a parent who does not have custody of his child is simple: What you do now should be whatever is in the best interest of your child. I am not indifferent to your wants and needs. It will be well if they can be supplied. But at this stage, your dominant consideration must be the interest of your child. He is the innocent victim of what is happening. He stands in the position of greatest danger in this whole affair. His character and personality are still in the formative stage. Nothing can prevent his being hurt by what has transpired. Every possible effort must be made to minimize the hurt, however, and to make it possible for him to develop into a normal, healthy, mature adult.

Parent Without a Partner

As a divorced parent with custody of your child, can you give your child a normal homelife?

"A normal homelife" is generally assumed to be essential to the healthiest emotional development of a child. In our minds "normal homelife" means two parents and their children living in a community where most of the neighbors are also two parents and their children.

One-parent families, however, have always been a part of the American scene. During periods of war, by the tens of thousands men have been taken away from their families for indefinite periods of time. In war and peace, young widows and widowers by the thousands rear their children alone. In smaller numbers, but significant nevertheless, unmarried mothers rear their own children. With the rising divorce rate, formerly married parents are becoming, if not commonplace at least not unusual.

How do the children of such one-parent homes fare? Specifically, how do the children of divorced parents fare? Are the chances increased that the child of divorced parents will become a problem to society?

A clue to the answer to this question can be found in the area of juvenile delinquency. One study of approximately eighteen thousand juvenile delinquents revealed that only about 10 percent of the delinquent boys and 20 percent of the girls were children of divorced parents.[5] These figures do not tell the whole story. Obviously the best environment in which a child can grow up is a happy home with two parents present. Yet "the largest proportion of these children who fall foul of the law come from families which are emotionally broken,

without having their disharmony overtly recognized by a re-
course to law." [6] *The fact that you are divorced,* in other
words, *does not in itself increase the prospects that your child
will be delinquent.* Indeed, your divorce may have reduced
that prospect by removing your child from an environment
that was seriously disturbing.

As you face the prospect of rearing your child without the
help of his father or mother, you will do well to keep one
fact in mind: Your child's needs are exactly the same as the
needs of all other children. He needs food, clothing, and shelter.
He needs to love and to be loved. He needs friends. He needs
adult models from whom he can learn what it means to be
a man and what it means to be a woman. He needs an education.
He needs a right relationship with God. Your problem is to
supply those needs without the help of your husband or wife.

In addition to these normal needs, however, your son or
daughter may have some special problems. One of these is
a complication in the area of role identification. Children learn
from the adults around them what it means to be a man or
a woman. They learn, primarily from their parents, how men
and women treat each other. As they see their father and mother
in the give and take of family relationship, they learn what
the roles of husband and wife are. Now they must learn this
without seeing it operative in their own home.

Another special problem is the emotional scars which your
child may bear from his observation of and perhaps participation
in the conflict that led up to your divorce. As we have seen,
each child responds to life in his own way. Yet your child
cannot help having been affected. You must help him deal
with his hostilities, fears, guilt, anxiety, frustration, and the
like.

If your divorce has resulted in your moving into a new
residence, your child faces an additional difficulty. As he is

adjusting to the absence of his father or mother, he is also having to make adjustments in almost every other aspect of his life: the place where he lives, his friends, his church, his school. A move is almost always an emotionally trying experience, even for adults. A move at this time may compound your child's insecurity.

As you try to deal with your responsibilities, you probably will feel great pressure. Not only do you have to combine the roles of father and mother; you have to do it while you are trying to earn a living. In addition, you will have the entire responsibility of operating your household. You may soon feel that you simply do not have enough time or enough energy or enough emotional strength.

Can you do it? Already you have one thing going for you. However difficult the present situation may seem, at least your home is now free of the tensions that characterized it before your divorce. No longer are you in the never-never land of being physically together but emotionally separated. Now you can concentrate on building that good life for yourself and your child.

A number of resources are available to you in your effort to rebuild your life and to help your child rebuild his. As a Christian, you have the spiritual resources of faith. You know the effectiveness of private prayer and of corporate worship. You know that the church is a "spiritual home" for you and for your child. Participate fully in the life of the church and make it possible for your child to share in those church activities planned for him. There he can find that religious education, that worship, and that contact with friends that will help him adjust and will help him mature.

You may also turn to other adult members of your family for help. Your parents or your brothers and sisters may be able to supply to an extent those models of adult behavior that your child needs. An uncle cannot be a father. Yet he may do some things that otherwise a father might do. Though a grandparent is always a grandparent, a grandmother can be a "mother figure." Your family will have their normal responsibilities which they must not neglect. If they are nearby, however, they might be happy for the opportunity to help you and your child.

A national organization of "Parents Without Partners" was established in 1957. If there is a local group in your town, you might do well to contact them. They have a variety of programs in which concerned individuals provide some of the contacts which children need with adults. While the programs vary from one town to another, nearly all of the local chapters conduct recreational activities for groups of children under the supervision of adults. These programs are especially helpful for preschool-age children whose contacts with adults are quite limited.

Another resource is the school. If your child is of school age, he may find a teacher, or several teachers, who will help meet his special needs. If that happens, do not be jealous. Rather be grateful that other adults are able and willing to help your child.

What I have said thus far is that your task is a big one and that you should be willing to utilize every available resource in your effort to fulfill it. In the event, however, that either you or your child seems not to be handling the situation adequately, another option is open. You might benefit from consulting with your minister or with a professional counselor. While not every minister is a trained counselor, many are. Many others without such training nevertheless have enough experience and insight to make them sensitive to your needs and capable of helping you understand yourself in your present situation.

Whatever you do in building a new life for yourself and your child, you are going to have to invest two things that are probably limited: time and money. Since these two vital elements are in short supply, spend them wisely and well. Be sure that you devote them to things that really matter. Which is more important *at this moment*, cleaning the house or playing with your child? Being with your friends or being with your child? Clothes for your child or books for your child? Both you and your child have needs, and sometimes those needs may seem to conflict. What can you give up for your child? What should you insist on for yourself?

All of this means that you need a balance in what you expect from your child. You may well expect his cooperation. You are now both father and mother, breadwinner and housekeeper. You cannot do both everything that you once did and everything that your ex-mate once did. It is not unreasonable to insist that your child perform whatever household responsibilities he is capable of at his age. If he is old enough to keep his own room in order or to help with the housecleaning or to help with the preparation of meals and washing the dishes, he should be expected to do so. Your child is not an adult and should not be saddled with adult responsibilities. He should not be expected to perform his chores with the skill of an adult. Yet he can rightly be expected to help *at the level of his own capabilities.*

You will do well to learn some new skills so that you can do for your child some of the things that your ex-mate once did. There is no reason that a father cannot learn to sew on buttons or to iron dresses and shirts or to care for cuts and scratches. There is no reason that a mother cannot learn to repair a bicycle or to throw a ball. Either a mother or a father should be able to pray with a child, to answer his questions about life, to reassure him about his fears and worries. Indeed, these chores may be some of those things that a parent will find both most helpful and most rewarding.

Although this is not always the case, you may be able to count on a good deal of help from your ex-mate. When a mother is given custody of a child, the father is usually required by law to contribute to the support of his child. (The time may come when fathers who have custody may count on the mother contributing to the support of her child!) Such requirements often are extremely difficult to enforce, and unfortunately a mother sometimes finds herself with the sole financial responsibility. Although child support payments are usually a financial burden for the one who has to make them, they should be paid regularly. Otherwise the child's needs may not be adequately met. Indeed, when crises arise, such as medical problems or special educational needs, a father might be expected to do more than make the required monthly payments. After all, a divorce does not terminate a man's responsibility for his child.

Other help than financial is both possible and desirable. If you and your ex-mate can be polite to each other and can discuss frankly the needs of your child and plans for meeting those needs, your child will fare much better. Together the two of you should make decisions on such important matters as your child's health, his schoolwork, his participation in religious activities. Together you should decide about and provide for such special things as music lessons, membership in youth organizations, and summer activities. Since the two of you apparently had difficulty cooperating before your divorce, it may seem unrealistic to expect such cooperation now. Yet perhaps the two of you learned something from your past failure. Since you are both concerned about your child, you should make the necessary effort to work together.

Notes

1. J. Louise Despert, *Children of Divorce* (New York: Doubleday, 1962), p. vii.

2. Earl A. Grollman, *Explaining Divorce to Children* (New York: Beacon, 1969), pp. 25-26.

3. Mindey, *op. cit.*, p. 98.

4. *Ibid.*, p. 100.

5. Cited in Despert, *op. cit.*, p. 116.

6. *Ibid.*

7. YOUR DIVORCE AND THE LAW

Divorce is a legal action.

Because the termination of a marriage involves a whole complex of personal, social, and religious considerations, it is not simply a legal settlement. Unavoidably, however, the divorce process is handled in the courts.

So far as the law is concerned, marriage is a legal contract. Two people who enter into that contract do so in a manner prescribed in the law. Having entered into that contract, they have taken upon themselves certain responsibilities in the anticipation of receiving certain benefits.

Divorce is the legal termination of a marriage contract. It restores the parties to the marriage to the status of single persons. It frees them of the obligations of their marriage and it deprives them of the benefits. Just as they had to meet certain legal requirements for the formation of their marriage, so are there legal requirements for the termination of that marriage.

In reality, you can never be restored to your premarital state. The things that have happened to you have changed you, not only emotionally but also legally. Your disentanglement from your marital partnership is far more complicated than it seems on the surface. You will do well to consider carefully the process by which you have reached this point in your life and what are the implications for your future.

The Legal Approach

"The law of divorce," says Robert Sherwin, "was written on the assumption that since marriage was something that no man was supposed to put asunder, putting it asunder should be made as difficult as possible." [1]

In a sense, the law seems to treat divorce as a penalty for wrongdoing. One party has to sue the other for divorce—so that there is a "plaintiff" and a "defendant." The plaintiff sues on some ground: he charges the defendant with some violation of the marriage contract. Even if both parties to the marriage want a divorce and work out all sorts of arrangements in advance, the process is the same.

The process seems a maze of technicalities and delays. It begins with the filing of a complaint naming both parties, stating the charges against the defendant, and citing the relief sought by the plaintiff. Once filed, the complaint becomes a part of the public record and is open to anyone who wishes to find out anything about it. The defendant is notified of the action and informed that he must answer the complaint within a specified period of time.

If a divorce is contested, the proceedings may stretch out over several months and the expense in money and time and emotion may be quite great. If it is not contested, it may be settled in a matter of days. In either event, it is settled by means of a "trial."

Because it makes the process so difficult, the law would seem to be against divorce. Superficially it appears that the state tries to prevent people from terminating their marriage by making it easier for them to be reconciled than it is for them to get a divorce. Exactly the reverse effect often results, however. The whole process militates against reconciliation and intensifies the hostilities of people who have become estranged from one another. The charges and countercharges, which seem 'to accompany nearly all cases, really make matters worse.

Furthermore, the system almost forces people who are intent on divorce to perpetrate a fraud. In every state the law specifies the grounds on which one person can sue another for a divorce. The complaint, therefore, is not likely to state the real reason for seeking a divorce but rather some ground on which a divorce can be won in the state where the action is filed. For many years the most common grounds have been cruelty (either physical or mental) and desertion. In recent years, however, more and more states have been granting divorce on the basis of separation for a specified length of time, and this is fast becoming the most common ground. Divorce on this last ground is the nearest thing to "divorce by mutual consent" recognized in this country.[2]

You may have discovered that in general women have the upper hand in the divorce court. Since they are still regarded as "the weaker sex," the courts are generally more sympathetic to them. Even though both parties probably share in the responsibility for the failure of the marriage, it is easier to place the blame on the man. There are more grounds on which a woman may sue a man for divorce (grounds such as "nonsupport") or is more likely to do so (grounds such as "cruelty"). Furthermore, the courts generally seem to show more sympathy for a woman in a bad situation. Even though both parties may want the divorce, therefore, it is far more common for the woman to be the plaintiff than for the man. Indeed, about three fourths of all divorces are granted to women.

The obvious purpose of a divorce is to sever a marital relationship. More is involved than that, however. That result can be secured by a simple separation. A man and a woman can simply stop living as husband and wife, with everything that is involved in that relationship, simply by taking up separate residences. All of the necessary arrangements can be worked out without going to court. A divorce is necessary, however, to ensure that the rights of everyone are protected and that in the future the two persons can function as single individuals. All of the legal involvements must be brought to an end in such a way that the two persons are indeed free.

The Separation

If you are separated but not yet divorced, you need to be quite careful about your legal situation.

The law does not require a husband and wife to live together. In the eyes of the law, however, separation is not a simple process. You may think that you are "separated," only to find yourself charged with desertion! Or with nonsupport! Or you might find yourself deprived of the right to support!

Robert Sherwin describes a situation that, though hypothetical, is quite possible:

Without advice of counsel they [H. and W.] separate. For a short time, the relief of not being forced to deal with each other vis-a-vis, day after day, is so great that both parties fail to realize that, like anything else, a separation cannot be left hanging in midair. W., the wife, has remained in the marital domicile and suddenly panics when the rent comes due and there is insufficient money to pay it in her checking account. Nothing specific was discussed by H. and W. before H. left. He had merely assured W. that all would be taken care of. When the panic sets in, emotional fuses blow, and quite literally, all hell breaks loose. W. rushes into family court, with or without an attorney, demanding support. H., with an attorney, comes into court, and very innocently explains to the judge that he recognizes his obligation to support his wife and indeed wishes to support his wife, but will do so only if, in fact, she will allow him to live with her. He carefully relates to the judge how he was asked to leave in no uncertain terms, and says that, as far as he understands the law (with the help of his attorney), he has done nothing to entitle his wife to force him to leave. If the wife wishes to state that the separation was a voluntary one on the part of both parties, since both parties had agreed to divorce each other, she will be horrified to discover that to agree to divorce is illegal and against public policy in every jurisdiction in the United States. . . . Thus the wife has the choice of either returning to a sick marriage or remaining separated (but not divorced) without support from her husband.[3]

Sherwin adds that the husband's problem is that the courts might interpret as abandonment or desertion what he had thought was a voluntary separation by mutual consent. All of this means that if you have separated, you will do well to have legal advice.

Legal separations are not final. They do not always result in divorce. Sometimes a couple use separation as a trial period to discover whether they really want to end their marriage. Many decide that they do not want to be divorced but instead want to try again to make a success of their marriage.

More often, however, legal separation is the first step in the divorce process. In a sense, since all normal marital relationships cease, it *is* a divorce which only lacks legal formalization. The proceedings in the court, and the negotiations leading up to those proceedings, merely unravel the legal ties. If you are in this state, you need a carefully worked out separation agreement, handled by your attorney.

In general, in a separation agreement you do not agree to divorce. You may, however, recognize that in the future one or the other of you might seek a divorce. The importance of this distinction lies in the fact that arrangements you make at the time of your separation are not binding in the divorce action. If the separation agreement is well-written, it may serve as the pattern for the terms of the divorce. Such is not necessarily the case, however. If the agreement is illegal, or if its conditions endanger the health, safety, and welfare of your children, the court may make other arrangements.[4]

For your own self-protection, you should be extremely careful not to violate in any way the stated conditions of your separation. If you do, you might easily complicate the divorce proceedings. If in any way you interfere with the agreed-upon rights of the other party, that interference may become a factor in important decisions related to your divorce.

During this period you will do well to remember that legally you are still married. This fact should have a bearing upon your decision about whether to date other people. Although the law does not say so, it is generally understood that married people do not date other persons. Any dating activity now, therefore, might become a consideration in the settlement of your case in the courts and a consideration to your disadvantage. This is particularly true if you are dating a person whom later you may marry.

What do the two of you have the right to expect of each other during the period of separation? For one thing, you have the right to be left alone. If you have separated in order to think things through, you have resorted to this step because you have found that you cannot do it while you are living together. You have stepped out of the situation in order to try to look at it as objectively as possible. You cannot do that if your former mate is trying to influence your thinking.

The same thing is true if you have already decided that you are going to be divorced. As we have seen, the decision is a painful one at best. Having made it, however, you will intensify the problems of all concerned if you carry on the conflict with your spouse. There is no point in further alienating either children or friends from your former partner. Only harm can come to you and to your spouse if you carry on the battle.

That is not to suggest, of course, that you can avoid all contact. Together you will have to work out details related to your divorce. If you have children, you will have to maintain some kind of contact for a long time to come. If you continue to live in the same community, you will hear of each other—and perhaps even be asked about each other. You may see each other in public places—at church, at social gatherings, on the street. You owe it to each other to make all such contacts as painless as possible.

Another thing that you have the right to expect of each other during the period of separation is access to your children. In the long run the court will decide who will have custody of the children and what will be the visitation rights of the one who does not have custody. In the meanwhile, however, unless it is positively dangerous for your children, both of you should have some contact with them. However strong your distaste for each other now, neither of you should be deprived entirely of your parental role.

Both of you also have the right to some consideration in the matter of property arrangements. That too will ultimately be decided in the court. In the meantime, however, the one who leaves the residence, as well as the one who remains, needs furniture and transportation. There are regular financial obligations associated with the operation of the household which were incurred by both of you, and in which both should share. Each of you has the right to expect some help from the other in such matters.

Making Sure Your Divorce Is Legal

Since divorce is the legal termination of a marriage, you might assume that once you have a divorce decree the matter is settled. Such is not necessarily the case, however. Three different types of divorce decrees are handed down. The most common type is the absolute divorce which does in fact completely sever the marital relationship and restore the individuals legally to the status of single persons. Persons so divorced are free to remarry immediately if they choose to do so.

In some states, *interlocutory* decrees are sometimes issued. Such a decree means that after the expiration of a specified length of time (usually a year), the individual may secure a final divorce decree. In the meantime he is not divorced but only separated. He is still legally married. He is not automatically divorced at the expiration of the specified period of time. Acting through his attorney, he may now take the initiative to get an absolute divorce. Usually he signs an affidavit to the effect that no reconciliation has been effected, that during the interlocutory period he and his spouse have not lived together, and that they have complied with all the requirements specified in the interlocutory decree. Under those conditions an absolute divorce may be granted without further court action.

Some states make provision for "limited divorce," or what is sometimes called "divorce from bed and board." In such cases legal provisions are made for the couple to live apart, although their marriage is not terminated in the sense that they are restored to the status of single persons. They are not free to marry someone else. This may seem a marital "limbo," for it sounds as if the couple are neither married nor single. There are good reasons for such an arrangement, however. For people who find that they can no longer live together but whose religious convictions prohibit divorce, this may be a helpful solution to their problem. It both protects the legal rights of the parties involved and respects their religious convictions.

The majority of all divorces granted in the United States today are uncontested. That is, the defendant in the action accepts the service of the legal papers but intentionally does not within the prescribed time answer the complaint. On the day of the trial he does not defend himself against the charge.

He admits his guilt, in effect, by failing to act. The decision is then at the discretion of the judge. He may grant the divorce, as he usually does. Or he may decide that the complaint has not been adequately proved and deny the divorce.

Although your divorce may be uncontested, it is not necessarily amicable. Indeed, most uncontested divorces are not. Rather, they are full of charges and countercharges. They are characterized by each individual trying to get for himself the best possible arrangement, without much regard for what happens to the other. Apparently the only thing they can agree on is that they both are anxious to have the marriage terminated.

If your divorce is uncontested, working through your attorneys, the two of you will come to some agreement on a number of matters that must be settled before the trial. The arrangements may be made final in the judge's chambers, with the judge being the arbiter on such matters as child custody and visitation rights, support, property settlement, and so on. The trial, then, is simply a formal judicial hearing in which the judge determines whether there is a legal ground for divorce and whether the final settlement is fair and reasonable.

In this connection a word should be said about "migratory" divorces. Because it is easier to obtain a divorce in some states than in others, many people establish residence in a given state in order to be divorced there. One has to live in Nevada, for example, for only six weeks to become a citizen of that state. As a resident of Nevada, he is then free to sue for divorce there. If his spouse is properly represented in court by attorney, there usually are no problems. Divorce in hand, he can then return to his home state as a single person. His divorce will be recognized as valid anywhere in the United States. The validity of the divorce is determined by the laws of the state where it is granted.

Ex parte divorces are another matter. If the defendant in

the proceedings did not appear in court, and if he was not represented by attorney, there may be complications. In this case the defendant did not merely default and thereby agree to the divorce. He was not involved in the action at all. The court had no way of knowing whether he was even aware of the proceedings. It is entirely possible that a divorce secured under these circumstances may not be recognized in states other than the one where it was granted.

If your divorce is contested, the situation can be a difficult experience for everyone involved. The courtroom proceedings are much like any other trial. The order of procedure is the same, the rules of evidence are the same, and the treatment of witnesses is the same. The chief difference lies in the fact that the case will be heard by a judge sitting without a jury. As Walter T. Winter says, this kind of trial contains "the emotion of personal defeats, heartbreak, disappointment, unhappiness and despair. The principals in such actions, almost without exception, find them to be an ordeal, not entertainment." 5

Disentanglement

If your divorce were simply a matter of the two of you taking up separate residences, it might be a simple matter. As husband and wife, however, you have been legal partners in many ways. You have owned property together. You have assumed certain joint financial obligations. You have been jointly responsible for taxes. Both of you have obligations to your children. The legal disentanglement of such matters can be quite complicated.

Property Settlement

One of the most common legal problems in divorce is the fair and equitable distribution of property. Implementing such a settlement may require that certain property be sold or that one person buy the share which belongs to the other. It will become even more difficult if one of you insists that he has personally invested a great deal more than the other in the acquisition of that property. You will, of course, need the services of your attorney in working out a property settlement. It is well to decide these matters in connection with your legal separation.

Property settlements agreed upon at the time of separation are usually approved by the court and made a part of the divorce decree. Such is not always the case, however, and you should not assume that it will be so in your situation. If your agreement is not carefully worded, some new dispute might arise over differing interpretations. Furthermore, in the interest of justice or to protect the rights of your children, the courts might modify certain portions of your agreement. A man might agree to a generous property distribution, for example, in return for his wife's agreement to low child-support payments. It is entirely possible, however, that at a later date the court might order an increase in his support payments.

This insistence upon legal arrangements for property settlement might seem unnecessary since you are a Christian. After all, Christians are supposed to be fair and just in their dealing with all people—even with people whom they do not like. Can we not expect Christians who are divorcing to act responsibly even in this traumatic situation? The answer is that we may *not* expect that. A man and woman who have not been able to deal with each other in a Christian manner as husband and wife are no more likely to do so when they are separated.

Taxes

Your divorce significantly alters your tax situation. You will do well to acquaint yourself with the provisions made in the Internal Revenue Code for property settlements, alimony, and child support, for your status is now different.

For tax purposes, your marital status at the end of the taxable year determines your status for the entire year. If you are married at the end of the year, you are treated as if you were married throughout the year. If you are divorced at the end of the year, you are treated as if you were divorced throughout the year. If you and your spouse were living apart but not legally separated, you could file a joint return. But if you were divorced, even though your divorce was granted on the last day of the year, you cannot file a joint return.

A man who is required to make regular payments of alimony may claim those payments as deductions for income tax purposes, and his former wife must pay tax on them. Child support payments, however, are not deductible by the husband and are not taxable to the wife. Either a husband or a wife, but not both, can claim the exemption for a dependent. If both contribute to the child's support, only one can claim the deduction. To claim the exemption, you must contribute more than half of the cost of your child's support.

In addition to the income tax situation, your other tax responsibilities might be complicated by your divorce. Both state and local governments have a variety of types of tax, involving either income or property tax or both. You will do well to consult an attorney or someone in the appropriate governmental office to learn what are your obligations.

The Will

If you and your spouse have made a will, you should give attention to it immediately. Although there are some restrictions, and more in some states than in others, it is generally assumed that an individual has the right to determine what disposition will be made of his property at his death. If you have a will, your former partner is involved in it in some way. You will need to revise the provisions which you have made. You will naturally want to guarantee your child's inheritance rights even though you may not want your former partner to benefit from your estate. The only way to be sure that your wishes will be met in the event of your death is to make the necessary changes in your will.

Insurance

Many families carry some form of medical insurance. Your interest in the health of your children, and perhaps your responsibility for it, continues in spite of your divorce. If by virtue of your divorce you and/or your children are no longer protected, you should move quickly to secure adequate coverage.

Life insurance is of a different nature. Parents are legally responsible for the health care of their children and of one another. Life insurance, however, is something that one marriage partner gives to another, or that a parent gives to a child, because he chooses to do so. Its purpose is to provide for one's survivors in the case of death. Your former partner probably is named as the beneficiary of any policy which you own. You may now want to change that, and you may want to name your children as beneficiaries. If your children are named, however, and if they are under age at the time of your death, there may be serious complications in their receiving the money at the time when they need it most. The money may be held in trust for them until they reach the age of eighteen, or even twenty-one. It may be best for your former spouse to continue to be named as beneficiary so that she (he) may have the money to use on the children when they need it most.

Debts

It is a rare couple that has no debts at the time of their separation. What are your responsibilities for the debts of your former marriage partner? The laws vary from state to state, of course, and you may again need the advice of your attorney.

Some generalizations, however, may be helpful.[6]

First, almost all states have done away with the common law provision that at marriage a man becomes liable for the premarital debts of his wife. Because of their understanding of the nature of marriage, most people assume that at marriage the financial obligations of either become the obligations of both. Legally, however, neither is now held accountable for the premarital debts of the other.

Second, community property *may* be considered liable for premarital debts. When the debts are the man's, such is the case in every state except Arizona and Washington. Only in California and Texas, however, may a creditor proceed against community property to make settlement for a woman's premarital debts.

Third, a man generally cannot be held accountable for his wife's debts unless those debts were contracted for the necessities of life.

Finally, after divorce neither husband nor wife is in any way liable for the debts incurred by the other.

Custody

If you have children, the custody of those children is one of the thorniest issues with which you have to deal. It may prove to be the most difficult problem for the court to handle. We have already discussed the emotional aspect of this problem. At this point we need to be clear on the legal situation.

Legally, to be given custody is to be given the responsibility for the health, welfare, and safety of a child. That responsibility may be defined in a variety of ways. If you have total custody, though your child's other parent may have visitation rights, decisions about the conditions of your child's life are yours to make. Sometimes, however, the court will approve a joint custody agreement, whereby the child spends part of his time with his father and part with his mother. Again, if you have more than one child, you may have custody of one but not the other. Sometimes arrangements are made for temporary custody, so that one spouse might have his child for a month or so each year, though the other has him for the rest of the time.

You should remember that custody settlements are always open to change. The parent who does not have custody, or some other relative, or even an unrelated individual may appear in course as a "friend of the child," and petition for a change in custody. The court may grant such a request if the current arrangements are not operating in the interest of the child. Furthermore, if the parent who has custody dies, the court makes a new decision. The child does not automatically come under the custody of his other parent. The new decision is based on the same considerations as the first one: In these circumstances, *what is best for the child?*

In the last resort, the court has final jurisdiction over your child. This was true even before you were separated from your spouse. Where husband and wife are living together and not contemplating divorce, the courts may, under certain conditions, conclude that it is to the best interest of a child that he be removed from the custody of the parents. While this does not happen often, the court has the right to place a child either in a foster home or in an institution.

The popular belief that in divorce cases the natural rights of the mother are considered greater than those of the father is incorrect. Legally neither has a prior claim. The courts presume nothing about the parents in determining custody.

In reaching a decision, the courts are not concerned about awarding custody to one parent in order to punish the other for any kind of misconduct. The conduct of the parents may be a factor in the decision. A parent who is an alcoholic or who is sexually promiscuous or who is violent at home may be considered an unfit parent. The basis for the court decision, however, is not punishment but something entirely different.

The fundamental consideration in court decisions about custody is the welfare of the child. That consideration is more important than the rights of the parents. It may even override any agreement which you and your spouse have worked out in advance. The court might even conclude that the interests of your child will be best served by neither of you having custody.

In spite of the generalization that the welfare of the child is the basic consideration, many people believe that in reality the welfare of the child is often ignored. Some specialists have even suggested that in all divorce proceedings in which children are involved, in addition to the attorneys representing the husband and the wife, there should be an attorney representing the children. Often parents are so anxious to terminate their marriage as quickly as possible that they fail to consider all the implications for their children. In her haste to be rid of an undesirable husband, for example, many a wife has agreed to child-support payments far too small, and far smaller than the husband was capable of handling. If the child had been represented by an independent attorney, however, he could have called attention to the problem and insisted that it be properly handled. In spite of the lip service paid the idea that the child must be protected, in actual fact both parents and court often fail to do so.

We can generalize about what the courts *usually* do. In most instances, the courts do respect agreements which are worked out in advance by divorcing persons. If you and your spouse have made an agreement which is fair and reasonable and protective of the health, welfare, and safety of your children, the court will doubtless approve it and give it legal sanction.

If that agreement is to the disadvantage of your children, however, the court may work out a plan of its own. You will do well, therefore, to be sure that what you work out is mutually satisfactory and that it is scrupulously adhered to. It should be quite clear as to what are the rights and the obligations of both parents. It should be sufficiently flexible to take care of unforeseen circumstances. And it should be followed with a mutual trust and cooperation that apparently was impossible to the two of you in marriage!

In the majority of cases involving young children, the mother is given custody. This decision, it should be noted, is based upon custom rather than law. People simply assume that younger children belong with their mother. They assume further, that since he has to be out on the job earning money, a father is likely to have little time to spend with his child. As a matter of fact, however, a divorced mother probably will have to find employment, if she is not already at work, so as to meet all the financial obligations of operating a household by herself. In recent years, therefore, a divorced man's chances of getting custody of his young child have been increasing. If the decision has not yet been made about the custody of your child, you cannot assume that regardless of all else he will be with his mother. Do not simply rely on custom, therefore. Work out with your former spouse an agreement that is truly in the best interest of your child and the court will probably approve it.

In cases involving older children, custom is not nearly so unanimous. Often a child who is ready to go off to school, or nearly at that age, is placed under the custody of the father. In the case of high school age children, daughters are sometimes assigned to their mother and sons to their father. Furthermore, often the wishes of the children themselves are taken into consideration.

In making its custody decision, the court may specify certain conditions that must be met. If, for example, your child has special health problems, the court may name the physician under whose care he is to be placed. It may require that he be sent to a special school or that he be given special training. The court is not likely to impose any religious requirements, however, and in fact is unlikely to enforce any agreement about religion which you and your former spouse have made.

Unless there are other considerations that make it disadvantageous to your child, the court may be counted on to give visitation rights to the parent who does not have custody. Every attempt will be made to work out a "reasonable" arrangement. It is to the advantage of everyone concerned—father, mother, and child—that the two of you, insofar as possible, agree as to what is reasonable and that you try in every way to make the arrangement a happy one for everyone. Like any other order of the court, this visitation right is legally enforceable. The parent having custody may lose that custody if this provision is violated.

A word of warning is in order here. Visitation rights and support payments should not be used in a continuing battle between you and your former spouse. The person who withholds payments in order to secure a better deal on visitation may be held in contempt of court. On the other hand, the refusal of the visitation rights to force payment of delinquent support installments is also a violation subject to prosecution. The enforcement of the conditions, in other words, is a matter to be handled by the court, not by the parties to the divorce. The court may suspend visitation rights until payment is made; or the court may suspend payment until visitation is permitted.

Alimony

For a long time it has been assumed that it is the responsibility of a man to support his wife. The concept of alimony is based on the idea that that obligation continues even though a man and his wife dissolve their marriage. The term "alimony" is sometimes used to refer both to a man's payment to his former wife and to his payment for the support of his children. At this point, however, we are referring only to the payment to the wife.

There are two classes of alimony: temporary and permanent. Temporary alimony is that which is paid before a divorce case comes to trial. Courts sometimes allow it to sustain a wife and to pay her costs in the suit until the issue is settled. They are unlikely to allow it, however, if she brings the suit against her husband and the court is not sure that she has a good case. Neither are they likely to allow temporary alimony if she has ample means to support herself and to pay her fees.

Permanent alimony is determined by the court in connection with the final settlement of a case. Ordinarily it is an amount to be paid regularly as long as the man lives or until the woman remarries. The provision for the payment of alimony is subject to modification when conditions change.

In two states, North Carolina and Pennsylvania, permanent alimony is rarely ordered. The courts in those states assume that a husband's obligations to his former wife are ended by divorce. In the states where alimony is common, several factors are usually involved in the determination: the continuing needs and responsibilities of the wife, the duration of the marriage, the living standard of the couple during their marriage, the present economic resources of both husband and wife, the prospective earning power of both, the age and health of both, and questions of blame in the marital difficulty.

The decision which the court makes on the basis of all these considerations may be satisfactory to no one. Except in the case of people who have no money problems, the payment is not likely to be enough to support the wife. Yet it is likely to be so large that it will be a burden on the man to pay it. The simple fact is that two households cannot be operated as cheaply as one.

It should be observed that the requirement that a man pay alimony rests upon two assumptions: (1) that a man is responsible for the support of his wife; and (2) that a woman's earning power suffers because of her marriage, primarily because the responsibilities of homemaking and child care have taken her out of the labor market for several years. In the light of the current emphasis on women's liberation and equality of opportunity, these assumptions are likely to be reexamined. It may be that in the not-too-distant future the payment of alimony will be an unusual requirement in divorce actions.

Child Support

Child-support payments differ from alimony in that they are for the benefit of the child, not for the support of the former wife. If you and your former marriage partner have worked out an agreement concerning the support of your child, the court probably will approve that agreement provided, in the judgment of the court, the provision is adequate. The court has a great deal of power when dealing with children, however. Even if you and your former spouse have agreed on what is to be paid for child support, the court may either increase or decrease that amount. If you have not come to some agreement, the court will determine on its own what is to be done. Furthermore, the court can make changes at any time until the child legally becomes an adult.

The payment of child support is not tied in with the question of whether a woman can support her child alone. Whatever her circumstances, the child's father has responsibilities which he cannot evade. He cannot plead insufficient income as an excuse for not helping support his child. The amount of his income is a factor in determining *how much* he may be required to pay, but not a factor in determining *whether* he is to pay anything. Support is his obligation.

The amount of support that a man must pay will be determined on the basis of the same factors considered in deciding the amount of alimony. As always, the court will be primarily concerned with the welfare of the child. And realistically, the court is not likely to require more than the man is capable of paying.

The person who pays the required child support is not entitled to receive an accounting of how the money is spent. A woman who has custody of her child is presumed to be capable of fulfilling her obligations properly. If it can be demonstrated that she is not doing so, and that the child is suffering some kind of neglect, she may lose custody. But so long as she has custody, she alone determines how best to care for the child.

For many women, one of the most serious problems after divorce is the collection of the child-support payments which her former husband was ordered to make. It is not unusual for a man to skip payments from time to time, or to make payments of less than the specified amount. If he does so, the courts may take action against him. His property and/or wages can be attached. He can even be sent to jail for his refusal to pay. The difficulty with these procedures, however, is that he may have no property to attach, and he may quit his job and move elsewhere.

In dealing with the question of the support of your child, whether you have custody or whether he is under the custody of his other parent, you must put first the needs of your child. Unless you are better off financially than most divorced parents, you will have a difficult time of it. A family income that was perhaps barely adequate before your divorce now has to be stretched somehow to support two households. If there was only one income, the mother may now have to go to work outside the home. That will involve added expense for child care. If both husband and wife worked before their divorce, there is little likelihood that their income can now be increased. The only alternative seems to be to find some way of cutting down on expenses. That is not impossible, for most of us have a rather high standard of living. It will be difficult, however, for most of us have become accustomed to and enjoy that high standard. The facts being what they are, however, there seems no other alternative.

Notes

1. Robert Sherwin, *Compatible Divorce* (New York: Crown, 1969), p. 19.

2. Note: In January, 1970, California's "no fault" plan for divorce went into effect. This plan may become the pattern for divorce legislation in the other states.

3. Sherwin, *op. cit.*, pp. 91-92.

4. *Ibid.*, pp. 291-92.

5. Walter T. Winter, *Divorce and You* (New York: Crowell-Collier, 1963), p. 74.

6. *Ibid.*, pp. 111-12.

8. REMARRIAGE?

"Dr. Crook, you don't know me, but I'd like to ask you a question," said the voice on the other end of the line. "Do you marry divorced persons?"

"I have performed marriage ceremonies for some divorced persons," was my answer, "and I probably shall do so again. But I always have at least one conference with a couple, divorced or not, before I agree to perform a marriage ceremony for them. Would you like to come talk with me about your situation?"

"Well, what would we have to talk about? I am ashamed of some of the things I have done, but I am a Christian now and all of that is over. Besides, the man I want to marry is divorced too, and he doesn't like people prying into the past."

"Since you are a Christian, may I ask why you don't want your own minister to perform the ceremony?"

"He says that because I am divorced, if I marry again I will no longer be acceptable to the church."

This young woman, with whom I talked at some length on the telephone but who never followed up on our conversation, had all sorts of problems in her plans to remarry. She was not sure that it was not a sin for her to remarry. She was eaten up with guilt about her past. She was planning to marry a man who was a poor marriage risk. She had no support from family or friends or church. She knew personally no minister or counselor with whom she felt she could discuss her situation. But she was going ahead nevertheless.

Sooner or later you are likely to come to grips with the question of whether you should remarry. You probably have nothing like the problems of my unknown caller. As you consider the matter, however, you will want to take into account not only personal but also sociological and religious considerations.

What Do Other People Do?

Failure in marriage, as signaled by divorce, apparently does not sour most people on marriage itself. In any given year, about one fourth of the persons who marry in this country have been divorced.[1] Indeed, divorced people in any age are more likely to marry than are persons who have never married. At the age of twenty-five, for example, a single woman has eighty-eight chances out of a hundred of marrying. The chances are ninety-nine out of a hundred, however, that her divorced friend will remarry. Of all divorced people, about two thirds of the women and three fourths of the men eventually remarry. Divorced men are generally in a greater hurry to remarry than are divorced women. Men divorced in their twenties are likely to marry again within two years; women divorced in their twenties are likely to remarry within three years. Women who have children are just as likely to remarry as those who do not, and they are likely to remarry just as quickly.[2] Whatever your age and sex, therefore, and whether you have children or not, the odds are very high that you will remarry.

Whom will you marry? A little more than half of the divorced persons who remarry marry someone who has also been divorced. Slightly more than a third of them marry people who have never been married. The rest marry persons whose first mate died.[3]

What are your prospects for success in your second marriage?

The relative success of the remarriages of divorced persons is a subject that needs a great deal more study. As yet we have developed no adequate criteria for measuring success in marriage. It is clear, however, that the risk of divorce in such marriages is significantly greater than is the risk of divorce in first marriages. The most important study of remarriages revealed that the divorce rate of second marriages in which either one or both partners had been divorced once before was more than twice as high as the divorce rate of persons in their first marriage.[1] Divorced persons, that is to say, are poorer marriage risks than are persons who have never married. That does not mean that your second marriage is doomed to failure. If 40 percent of the second marriages end in divorce, then apparently 60 percent are at least successful enough to remain together. What it does mean is that statistically your risk of failure is much greater.

Why the failure rate of remarried divorcees is higher we cannot say for certain. One reason may be that some people who want to be married are either unable or unwilling to make the personal adjustments necessary to success in marriage. A second reason may be that, due to pressure from family, friends, and even children, divorced persons often begin to date before they are emotionally ready for it, and consequently sometimes remarry before they have really adjusted to their previous failure. Still another factor may be a greater tolerance for divorce, or a greater willingness to resort to it, on the part of people who have already divorced once.

An element rarely considered in discussions of the relative success of second marriages, surprisingly enough, is what the people involved in such marriages think. Do they consider their second marriages better than their first? Goode found that 92 percent of the women involved in remarriages considered their second marriages either "better" or "much better" than their first.[5] Bernard found that in a large majority of cases the friends of remarried couples rated the second marriages as successful.[6] Of course, second marriages in which the couples were still together were being compared with earlier marriages that had ended in bitterness and conflict. By comparison they would be expected to show up quite well.

It seems, then, that we have two facts that appear to contradict each other. On the one hand, the divorce rate of remarriages is about twice as high as the divorce rate of first marriages. On the other hand, remarried divorcees see their second marriages as significantly happier than their first.

What do those successful second marriages have going for them? Bernard suggests three things. First, some people have learned from their failure. At the simplest level, they have learned in their first marriage some of the skills of housekeeping and economic arrangements and personal adjustments necessary in any marriage. At a more important level, they have developed a degree of maturity, wisdom, and tolerance in interpersonal relationships. Second, their failure in their first marriage has made them more determined to succeed in their second. They are all the more anxious to achieve the benefits of a stable family life. And third, they are older at the time of their second marriage. Since most of them are over thirty years of age, they are likely to have worked through the spirit of irresponsibility more characteristic of younger people.[7]

Women's Liberation and Remarriage

The Women's Liberation movement which came into being in the 1960s is directly and significantly related to the question of marriage—and therefore to the question of remarriage. It is a fact that from the beginning of our nation to the present the American woman has occupied a position of subordination to the American man. That subordination has been deeply ingrained in both custom and law.

Writing in 1963, Betty Friedan, the matriarch of women's liberation, compared American women to the inmates of Nazi concentration camps.[8] Perhaps that comparison is a bit over-drawn. Yet many women, cheered on by not a few men, have rallied round the cause of Women's Lib in a quest for equal educational, economic, and political opportunity. They insist upon their recognition as persons rather than as property, as individuals rather than as sex objects, as people with the right to choose what they shall be and do.

This right to choose is made difficult by the orientation of our society toward married people. Law, politics, business, education, religion—everything seems to assume that adults are married. If you doubt this, look at the tax break given to married people, the importance of the wives of politicians and business-men (noting, by the way, that politicians and business people are usually men), the kinds of professions into which women commonly go, and so on. Look, in fact, at the way the educa-tional program of your church is structured. Ours is a world organized by and for married people. This fact exerts a subtle pressure upon you to "try it again."

Women's Liberation, of course, is "different things to dif-ferent people." Its concerns range from the frivolous to the vital: from bra-burning to equal job opportunity and equal pay for equal work. At its best, however, it is concerned with the elimination of discrimination on the basis of sex in American life—in jobs, wages, education, and general involvement in all the affairs of life. It seeks to discover and to change all those mechanisms in the socialization process which prepare little girls for life in a male-dominated society and thus leads them to accept dependent adult roles.

Women's Liberation is championed by both men and women. It is also opposed by both men and women. Whether you favor it or oppose it, however, its effects are being felt. One of the effects is a decrease in the pressure upon women to marry. The unmarried woman, whether she is never-married or divorced, is much freer to make her decision about marriage on valid grounds rather than simply yielding to the pressure of society. To put it more bluntly: No longer does a woman have to have a man to be at home in our society.

For a man who wants to remarry, the situation is becoming more complicated. No longer can he count on any woman he marries fitting into the traditional role of a wife and mother who is subordinate to her husband. As women achieve the objectives of the liberation movement, they become harder to live with. When the stability of a marriage depended chiefly upon the subordination of one person to another, success was fairly easily achieved. Since those roles are no longer taken for granted, however, and harmony in marriage depends upon the adjustment of two independent persons to each other, it is much more difficult to achieve. Men are being forced to revise their expectations.

In the long run, however, the woman who is harder to live with may be the best kind of marriage partner. Even in the more patriarchal pattern of man-woman relationships, most people who had a truly successful marriage understood that it was a mutual achievement and that its success depended upon mutual love and respect and a division of labor which capitalized upon the strengths of both partners.

In any new marriage into which you enter, therefore, success of adjustment may be much more difficult to achieve. Almost certainly, however, the adjustment of two equals to each other will be far more rewarding than the subordination of one person to another.

Children and Remarriage

An important consideration in thinking about remarriage

is the effect that your marrying again would have upon your children. Unfortunately, however, we do not have much sound information on which we can base any generalization. Few studies have been made, and the evidence is at best confusing and at worst conflicting. The most that we can say is that children seem to be happiest and to mature best in happy and unbroken homes, that they have greater adjustment problems in reconstituted homes (that is, homes created by second marriages), and greatest problems in unhappy but structurally intact homes. This means that you may have done the best possible thing for your children by getting them out of a destructive home situation.

As to whether children are better off in one-parent homes or in homes reconstituted by remarriage, the evidence is even more scanty. Apparently, however, there seems no significant difference. The fact that you remarry will not guarantee your children a better homelife; neither will the fact that you remain unmarried assure them of a good life.

If this be the case, it would seem that your decision to divorce your spouse was one of vital importance to your children. Your decision about whether to remarry will not in itself be the determining factor in whether they will be well-adjusted. This decision, therefore, can well be based on other considerations.

Religion and Remarriage

What other people think and do is important to you because you are a part of society. You are subject to all of these considerations which we have been discussing, and often without even being aware of it you are influenced by them.

As a Christian, however, you find another consideration to be even more important than the pressures of society: What is the *right* thing to do?

The Scripture

We have seen (chapter 4) that Jesus insisted that marriage was intended by God to be a permanent relationship. We saw also that he dealt forgivingly and redemptively with all people who failed to achieve any ideal. Although we have no recorded instance of his dealing with divorced persons, we concluded that he would not treat them differently.

We have to face now the question of whether your remarrying would be a violation of the teaching of Jesus. At the outset, we must understand that what Jesus said about remarriage he said within the context of his teaching about divorce. Since all four Gospel reports of this teaching (Matt. 5:31-32; 19:3-9; Mark 10:11-12; Luke 16:18) agree in the statement about remarriage, we can base our discussion on one only:

And he said to them, "Whoever divorces his wife and marries another, commits adultery against her; and if she divorces her husband and marries another, she commits adultery" (Mark 10:11-12).

Note that Jesus' reference to divorce and his reference to remarriage come in the same sentence. The implication may be, therefore, that a man must not divorce his wife *in order to marry another woman.* If this be the case, then the offense with which Jesus is concerned is the destruction of a marriage by involvement with another woman. He does not say anything about two unmarried people entering into a marital relationship. It seems clear that what he was concerned about was the termination of a marriage that had been contracted, not about the conditions under which a new marriage might be contracted.

If this interpretation is correct, then Jesus did not discuss the question of whether a divorced person could be remarried. We are probably reading too much into what he said if we interpret this passage as a prohibition of remarriage. It is entirely consistent with what he said to assume that a marriage which has been ended, whether by divorce or by the death of one of the marriage partners, would not in itself constitute a barrier to the contracting of a new marriage.

Paul's report and interpretation of the teaching of Jesus about marriage (1 Cor. 7:10-11) involves another important consideration. Paul said:

> To the married I give charge, not I but the Lord, that the wife should not separate from her husband (but if she does, let her remain single or else be reconciled to her husband)—and that the husband should not divorce his wife.

Note that Paul made this statement within the context of his discussion of the imminent return of Christ. In the light of that fact, he said, no one should change his status in life. Married people should remain married and single people should remain single. This fact explains Paul's parenthetical interpretation. He was not so much against remarriage as he was against *any* important change in one's status.

In the verses that follow, which he admits are his own interpretation, Paul continues to recommend that married people stay married. He recognizes, however, that a non-Christian might divorce his Christian spouse. "In such a case," said Paul, "the brother or sister is not bound" (1 Cor. 7:15). This statement clearly recognizes the possibility of the termination of a marriage. The implication of being "not bound" or "free" is that the conditions of the marriage no longer exist and that the individual is single.

In spite of his urging that people not change their status in life, Paul recognized the urgent drive toward marriage on the part of single people. He made the concession: "But if they cannot exercise self-control, they should marry. For it is better to marry than to be aflame with passion" (1 Cor. 7:9). Apparently Paul was talking about the passion of the sex drive. There are other powerful drives, however, which impel a person toward marriage. Those drives, furthermore, are not different in the never-married and the divorced, for the basic needs of human beings are the same.

Paul, then, was not concerned with discouraging divorced persons from remarrying. He was concerned rather with discouraging everyone from marrying in the circumstances of that day. It would seem that when he made the concession of permitting marriage to some, he was thinking of all unmarried persons, not just one class of them.

By way of summary: In the New Testament the ideal of marriage is presented as the permanent union of one man and one woman. To fail to achieve that ideal is to fall short of the purposes of God. People who have failed, however, are not by that failure cut off from God and from his purposes for them. It may be that in his providence, in spite of past failure, the achievement of that ideal is still open to you.

The Churches

Historically the attitude of the churches toward the remarriage of divorced persons has been negative. That, at least, has been the view reflected in official church teachings. Considering marriage a sacrament, the Roman Catholic Church has insisted that there can be no such thing as divorce (Canon 1118). So far as Catholics are concerned, the only thing that can terminate a valid and consummated marriage is death. Any Catholic who gets a legal divorce and marries someone else is, so far as the church is concerned, living in an adulterous relationship. That position still holds true.

In Protestant churches, for many years it was generally agreed that a divorced person could be remarried only if he were the "innocent party" to a divorce on the ground of adultery. In taking this position, the churches followed Matthew's report of the teachings of Jesus (5:31-32; 19:3-9) rather than Mark's (10:11-12) and Luke's (16:18). This was the officially stated position of the Methodists, the Presbyterians, the Lutherans, and the Episcopalians. It was also the unofficially stated position of most Baptists, Disciples, and other more loosely organized groups. Consequently many divorced persons who wanted to remarry found themselves in the position of not being able to be married in their church, and of not being able to be married by a minister. Those who sought out a minister often found themselves somewhat on the defensive as the minister tried to discover whether he could perform the ceremony.

In recent years most of the major Protestant denominations have significantly revised their regulations on the remarriage of divorced persons, and the process of revision is continuing to the present. The Lutheran Church in America, for example, in 1970 adopted a new "Social Statement" which says about remarriage:

When the question of the remarriage of a divorced man or woman arises, the church and the individuals themselves will do well to concentrate upon the potential of the new rather than the collapse of the former marriage. A clear understanding of the dynamics which led to the breakdown of the first union helps a person prepare more adequately for the second. A divorced man and woman, of course, should fulfill all legitimate obligations to the members of the broken family.[9]

The General Conference of the United Methodist Church adopted in 1972 a statement of "Social Principles" which included a section on "Marriage." For our purposes, the pertinent sentence is:

In marriages where the partners are, even after thoughtful consideration and counsel, estranged beyond reconciliation, we recognize divorce and the right of divorced persons to remarry, and express our concern for the needs of the children of such unions.[10]

The Protestant Episcopal Church revised its canons on marriage in 1973. The old canon, adopted in 1946, permitted a person who had been divorced for at least one year to apply to the Bishop for permission to remarry. The Bishop had thirty days for investigation, and if his investigation of the facts convinced him that "no marriage bond as the same is recognized by this church exists" he could give his approval for remarriage. It provided for the automatic excommunication for any person who remarried without this permission. The new canon, adopted in 1973, permits the divorced person to make his application thirty days after his divorce and eliminates the excommunication clause.

The *Book of Order* of the United Presbyterian Church in the United States of America provides that a minister asked to officiate at the marriage of a divorced person "may seek, for advice only, the review and counsel of his presbytery" [11] prior to making his decision about whether to officiate. The ultimate decision, therefore, is his to make.

Baptist ministers are not governed by any set of regulations. What they do about remarrying divorced persons is up to them. In the past, however, their views on remarriage have not been significantly different from those of their colleagues in other denominations. Although there has never been unanimity of opinion and action on this issue, it is quite probable that a significant number, perhaps most, would find themselves at home with the position represented by the new statements of the Lutherans, the Methodists, the Episcopalians, and the Presbyterians.

In addition to the more sympathetic view toward the remarriage of divorced persons, these new positions have another important emphasis in common: they all stress the responsibility of the church to minister with sympathy and understanding to people who want to try again in spite of their past failure.

If you wish to be remarried, you probably will find your minister anxious to help you begin your new union under the best possible of circumstances.

My own practice is an attempt to be faithful to the spirit and teaching of Christ, to help people confront themselves in their own situation, and to help them decide what is the best thing for them to do. I do not assume either that remarriage is wrong for everyone, no matter what the circumstances, nor that it is the right thing for anyone who wishes to try again. I am concerned about the prospects for success in the new marriage and for what failure or success in the new marriage will mean for the people involved. I am not interested in assessing responsibility for the failure of the first marriage, except insofar as it may have a bearing on what is to happen next. I consider the statistics that show that the failure rate of remarriages is twice that of first marriages to be important only insofar as they demand that divorced persons take carefully into account those things which suggest that their proposed marriage may have built into it the seed of failure. As in the case of first marriages, in other words, I am concerned about the formation of a marriage in which husband and wife, in harmony with God's purposes for them, can achieve a mutually satisfying and enriching experience, and in which children can have a home that will help them become well-adjusted and mature individuals.

In taking this kind of approach, I believe that I am acting on sound Christian principles. I know of no other area of life in which failure (which, after all, is a relative term) is allowed to prevent another attempt to achieve God's purposes. Jesus always met people where they were, took them at face value, and dealt with them redemptively.

As we have seen, forgiveness is a reality in connection with marital failure as in connection with anything else. And forgiveness is unconditional. The person who genuinely repents and seeks God's forgiveness receives it. That forgiveness removes all barriers between the individual and God. If you did incur guilt in connection with your previous marriage, and if you have sought God's forgiveness, then the record is clean.

This is not to suggest that you necessarily did incur guilt by divorcing your former spouse. The problem may have been in the formation of the marriage rather than in its dissolution. Or within the marriage problems may have arisen over which you had no control. In every failure in marriage two people are involved, not one. Both share in the responsibility for the failure. Yet often one does bear the greater responsibility than the other. If, in spite of your best efforts, your marriage failed, you need not be eaten up with guilt. And in this sense you do not need forgiveness for the failure.

If you should decide that for you remarriage is wrong, then the door is probably closed for certain kinds of social activities. You do not want to allow yourself to get into a situation where you have to choose between your conscience and marrying the person you love. If, on the other hand, you decide that it will not be wrong for you to remarry provided you find the right kind of partner, then you need to deal with a number of other questions of a personal nature.

The Personal Question

Why Get Married?

The fact that you are divorced does not in itself mean that the reasons that you wanted to marry to begin with no longer exist. You may have married at the time you did for inadequate reasons; or you may have married for adequate reasons, only to find that your marriage was a disappointment. Yet there are good reasons why most people want to marry, and it may be important for you to think about them now.

The obvious reason that people marry is that they are in love. It would seem that nothing else need be said.

Yet many people who are in love do not, for one reason or another, get married. And most people have already been in love with several other persons before they eventually marry. Many people who marry because they are in love "fall out of love" somewhere along the line. That is to say that love and marriage do not automatically go together. You *can* have one without the other.

When the question, Why get married? is pursued a little further, the word "happiness" usually creeps into the conversation. People marry because they expect that the union will make them happy. Yet it is hard to define this word and to discover what brings happiness. Most people, married or single, are sometimes happy and sometimes not. The condition fluctuates so much that it is apparent that happiness depends upon a great many factors, many of which are beyond the control of the individual or of the couple.

The mating urge is involved in the decision to marry. This urge is described in the biblical statement, "Therefore a man leaves his father and his mother and cleaves to his wife, and they become one flesh" (Gen. 2:24). While this urge focuses on the sex drive, it is not simply that. It is the yearning for personal fulfillment, for completion of the self by intimate companionship with a mate, for the perpetuation of the self through one's own children. Human beings have a hunger for a togetherness which can best be known within a rich and enduring personal relationship. This yearning is reflected in the statement, "It is not good that the man should be alone; I will make him a helper fit for him" (Gen. 2:18). Our deepest human need is to love and to be loved. However satisfying are our relationships with friends, they do not fully meet this need. Most people believe that only in the intimacy of marriage can they be fully accepted and only there can they give themselves without reservation.

If all of this was true of you before your marriage, your desire and your need have not been destroyed by the failure of that relationship. Indeed, that failure may have made you all the more determined to find success with someone else.

What Is Christian Marriage?

What a particular marriage is like depends upon many factors external to the union, and upon how the couple react to those factors. Consequently some marriages are happy, some are tolerable, and some are disastrous. None is likely to be ideal. The Christian ideal, however, may offer you a good perspective from which to consider the question of whether you should remarry.

Basic in the Christian ideal of marriage is the concept of unity. This concept is indicated in the phrase "one flesh" which Jesus borrowed from the Old Testament (Matt. 19:5; cf. Gen. 2:24). Paul also used this term in stating the ideal as he understood it (1 Cor. 6:15-16). The most apparent meaning of the phrase is a physical union. Since the physical is not isolated from the other elements of our nature, however, it is entirely proper to think of the words as signifying a union of the whole personalities. By God's grace two people, male and female, each with his own background and experience and personality and character, are made one. It is not a unity in which no distinctions remain. The man does not cease being himself, nor the woman herself. Since each remains an individual, there may be differences of opinion, of interests, of achievements. As a matter of fact, this unity is one in which the individuality of each is enhanced rather than destroyed. But it is nevertheless a relationship in which each becomes an integral part of the other.

With your first spouse you did not have this kind of unity.

Neither the law nor the marriage ceremony nor sexual intercourse nor your daily life achieved this result. As you consider remarriage, you need to assess the possibility of your achieving that kind of unity with someone else.

Closely related to the concept of unity is that of mutuality. Paul began his most comprehensive description of Christian family relationships (Eph. 5:21 to 6:4) with the exhortation, "Be subject to one another out of reverence for Christ." The rest of the passage indicates how each member of the family is to be subject to every other member. In the marriage relationship the wife is to "be subject to" the husband, and the husband is to "love" the wife. The patriarchal setting, clearly a factor in the description, is overshadowed by the reciprocal relationship of husband and wife. A real equality is implied, and the differences are differences of function rather than of worth or of importance. In this context, therefore, Paul talked about what each person owed to the other rather than about what each person might expect from the other.

As you consider your own situation, you need to decide whether you are capable of such mutuality, and whether the person whom you are contemplating marrying is capable of it. It is not easy. It is often beyond the power even of people who are in love with each other. This may have been one of the problems in your first marriage. Are you now capable of a way of life of which you were incapable then?

In biblical terms the husband-wife relationship is an exclusive one. The traditional marriage ceremony speaks in terms of "forsaking all others" and "cleaving only unto thee." If marriage is the kind of mutual commitment and unity that we have just spoken of, then it can involve only two people. There is something exclusive and unique between husband and wife. A person cannot commit himself in this way to more than one other person at the same time. The marital relationship thus allows for no competition and is in fact endangered when that possibility is kept open.

The natural concomitant of this exclusive unity is fidelity. Two people committed to each other in love are unlikely to have serious problems at this point. Negatively stated, infidelity is not so likely to be the cause of trouble between a husband and wife as it is to be the result of such trouble. Where the total marital relationship is good, and where the concept of commitment is taken seriously, the problem of infidelity is not likely to arise.

Should I Remarry?

In the last resort the question of remarriage is an individual one. The findings of the sociologists are informative and the generalizations formulated on the basis of these findings may be helpful to you. The teachings of Jesus and the position of the church are of great importance to you. You are not a statistic, however, and you cannot look at Christian teachings in the abstract. You are an individual using the best information available and committed to the highest ideals as you make a decision about your own course of action.

One question which you should ask of yourself is: Am I the kind of person who *should* or who *should not* be married? Long ago students of the family learned that some people can adjust to life successfully married but not single. Others can adjust successfully single but not married. Still others can adjust successfully either single or married. There may be a fourth category: people who cannot adjust successfully, whether married or single. It is important for you to know whether you are constitutionally capable of successful adjustment in marriage. If you are not, then you need go no further in your thinking about marriage. If you are, then there are other considerations to which you need to turn.

To answer this question, Should I remarry? you need to

take a long, hard look at yourself in the light of all that has happened. You need to ask such things as: Am I capable of fully trusting anyone? Can I open myself and reveal myself fully to anyone? Do I like myself? Do I like anyone else? Do I expect things to turn out well for myself? How well can I accept my own inadequacies? How well can I accept the limitations of another person? Why do I like the things that I do? Why do I choose the friends that I do? How do I regard the sex relationship in marriage?

Another area of concern should be the effect that your first marriage has had upon you. How badly hurt were you? Does it still hurt to think of some of the things that were said and done? Are there scars that make you an unsuitable partner for anyone else? Has your first partner warped your understanding of what it is to be a man or a woman?

You will need also to think carefully about the effect that another marriage will have upon your children. Will they resent someone else taking the place of their father or mother? Do they need someone in that position? At this point in their lives, will your remarriage make them happier and better adjusted?

If all of these questions suggest that for you remarriage is right, then you need to think carefully about the person whom you want to marry. What are the prospects for having with that person the kind of marriage you could not have with your first spouse? Are you agreed on religion? on basic objectives in life? on values? on attitudes? This is not the question of whether you love that person; it is assumed that if you are interested in marrying each other you are in love. But it is entirely possible, as you now know, to love someone with whom you could not have a good marriage. Love alone seems really to be unrelated to success or failure in marriage. The love that will make for success is the love for a person who has those qualities of character and personality that will complement yours, who has the same commitment that you have, and who can help you to be the kind of person you are capable of being.

Notes

1. Hugh Carter and Paul C. Glick, *Marriage and Divorce* (Cambridge: Harvard University Press, 1970), p. 82.

2. Richard Udry, *The Social Context of Marriage* (New York: Lippincott, 1971), p. 460; and William Kephart, *The Family, Society, and the Individual* (New York: Houghton-Mifflin, 1972), p. 470.

3. Ruth Shonle Cavan, *The American Family*, 4th ed. (New York: Crowell, 1969), p. 444.

4. Thomas F. Monahan, "The Changing Nature and Instability of Remarriages," Eugenics Quarterly, 5:78-85, 1958.

5. William J. Goode, *After Divorce* (Glencoe: The Free Press, 1956).

6. James Bernard, *Remarriage* (New York: Dryden, 1956).

7. *Ibid.*

8. Betty Friedan, *The Feminine Mystique* (New York: Dell, 1963), pp. 294-96.

9. "Social Statement of the Lutheran Church in America," adopted by the Fifth Biennial Convention, Minneapolis, Minnesota, June 25—July 2, 1970, p. 4.

10. "Social Principles of the United Methodist Church," adopted by the 1972 General Conference in Atlanta, Georgia, p. 7.

11. *The Book of Order,* 1972-73, 22:02, 42:28.

EPILOGUE

At best your divorce has been a difficult experience. It has meant the recognition of failure in the most important single undertaking of your life. It has meant that what you began with such high hopes and great expectations, and in the full blush of young love, has ended with disillusionment and frustration and even bitterness.

In your changed status you do not find yourself completely happy. Although you have improved your situation, you have not freed yourself of all your problems. As Carol Mindey put it, "The act of divorce usually solves nothing for an individual. You may sincerely believe you are getting rid of your biggest problem—your mate—only to discover your biggest problem was always you." [1] You have resolved one problem only to encounter others.

Problems, however, do not necessarily mean unhappiness and they do not necessarily indicate failure. In any circumstance life is full of problems—and those problems are opportunities. As you rebuild your life in new and different circumstances, you doubtless will make many mistakes. You will be living and working, however, in a situation which you believe you can handle. Now you live in hope rather than in despair. About one young divorcee Sandra Harvell said:

And Leigh says she has accepted the fact that even though she may not be living the best of all possible lives, this life is better than the one she did have. And more importantly, she says she has regained a hope that she had once lost—the hope that things can and will get better. [2]

As we have seen, divorce is sometimes a morally valid choice. It is that when it is the best possible way to deal with a situation that is dangerous and destructive for the marriage partners or for their children. It is that when it does more good than evil for all involved. It is that when nondivorce would involve serious consequences that would further warp and distort persons. If a poor marriage can be turned into a good one, then nondivorce is the best course to follow. But if the best evidence is that nondivorce will worsen rather than improve things, then divorce is moral.

By the same logic, as we have seen, remarriage is sometimes a morally valid choice. It is that when the second marriage holds promise of making the persons involved more complete and authentic human beings. It is that when it provides a happy and secure home in which children can mature and become well-adjusted persons.

Neither this judgment about divorce nor this judgment about remarriage ignores the teachings of the Scripture. Rather both judgments are based upon that fundamental concern in all of the teaching of Jesus: the total welfare of every individual as an object of the love of God.

Whether you choose to remarry or to remain single for the rest of your life, you are now looking to the future. Whatever you do, and however difficult may be the external circumstances of your life, you can face this future with confidence. You may have family who continue to love you and to give you emotional support. You may have old friends who stand by you, and you can count on forming new and meaningful friendships. You have the possibility of employment that is meaningful not only in terms of making money but also in terms of making a worthwhile contribution to your fellowman. You have the fellowship of your church and the inner resources of your own faith. You have the assurance that nothing "in all creation, will be able to separate us from the love of God in Christ Jesus our Lord" (Rom. 8:39).

Notes

1. Mindley, *op. cit.*

2. Sandra Harvell, "Four Divorcees Discuss Their Lives Now," *Raleigh Times.* January 12, 1972, p. 1-B.